Wanted → A Board Career

The Definitive Playbook for
Landing a Board Seat

Naomi Kent & Marlo Lyons

Copyright © 2026 by Naomi Kent and Marlo Lyons

All Rights Reserved. No part of this publication may be reproduced, stored in a retrieval system, or transmitted, in any form or by any means, electronic, mechanical, photocopying, recording, or otherwise, without the prior written permission of the publisher. Limit of Liability / Disclaimer of Warranty: The authors have used their best efforts in preparing this book and make no representations of warranties with respect to information accuracy or completeness of the contents of this book. Authors specifically disclaim any implied warranties of merchantability for fitness for a particular purpose. No warranty may be created or extended by sales representatives or written sales materials. The advice and strategies contained herein may not be suitable for your situation. You should consult with additional professional coaches or other professionals where appropriate. Neither the publisher nor the authors shall be liable for any loss of profit or any other personal or commercial damages, including but not limited to special, incidental, consequential, or other damages. Readers should be aware that internet web sites offered as citations and/or sources for further information may have changed or disappeared between the time this was written and when it is read.

Published in the United States by Future Forward Publishing, Scottsdale, AZ

ISBN: 978-1-7370181-9-3 (print)
ISBN: 979-8-9933546-0-6 (epub)
ISBN: 979-8-9933546-1-3 (audio)

Legal Disclaimer

The information contained in this book is the opinion of the authors and is based on the authors' personal experiences and observations. The authors do not assume any liability whatsoever for the use of or inability to use any or all information contained in this book and accept no responsibility for any loss or damages of any kind that may be incurred by the reader as a result of actions arising from the use of information found in this book. Use this information at your own risk. The authors reserve the right to make any changes deemed necessary to future versions of the publication to ensure its accuracy. Some names in this book have been changed to protect individuals' privacy.

Interior design and production by Dovetail Publishing Services
Editing by Matthew Gilbert
Jacket design by Jeff Zwerner

"An easy-to-read 'how-to' without ever being pedantic—well written, well organized, and truly comprehensive. I've never read a book that starts with 'why a board' and ends with 'onboarding and the work really begins.' It's a great playbook, and like all great playbooks, it leaves room for readers to apply their own talent and creativity."
— Stephanie Streeter, public, private and nonprofit board director and former CEO, Libbey Inc.

"A must-read roadmap for rising leaders who want a seat at the table."
— Alison Levin, Private board director, nonprofit board chair and president, NBCUniversal Advertising & Partnerships

"This is by far the most comprehensive guide to pursuing a board seat that I have seen in my 57 years of sitting on boards. If I only had this book over the years, I could have saved myself thousands of hours of explaining all this to good folks who were searching."
— Dennis Cagan, board chairman, board director and former public company CEO

"Essential reading for professionals ready to step into board service."
— Frank Jaehnert, Public company board member and former CEO Brady Corp.

"If I could offer advice to my younger self, beginning on my high school Key Club board, it would be to read this book. The lessons within would have saved me from many pitfalls and helped me contribute even more meaningfully along the way."
— Dennis Chookaszian, board director of more than 100 public, private, and nonprofit organizations and retired chairman and CEO, CNA Insurance Companies

"As a marketing executive, I appreciate frameworks that drive measurable outcomes. *Wanted → A Board Career* delivers. If you're serious about building a board career, this is the strategic playbook you need."
— Lesly Marban, board director and chief marketing officer

Contents

Foreword — vii

Preface — xi

Introduction — 1
   Common Board Career Myths — 2

Section I: DISCOVERY — 5

Chapter 1   **Why Join a Board?** — 7
   Determine Your Motivation — 8
   Identify and Define Your Values — 14

Chapter 2   **Who and What Makes a Great Board Member?** — 21
   Understand the Board Member Role — 21
   Board Member Attributes — 26
   Time Commitment — 30

Chapter 3   **Which Board Is Right for You?** — 33
   Types of Boards — 34
   Making Your Board Choice — 40

Section II: PREPARATION — 51

Chapter 4   **Preparing Your Brand** — 53
   Brand Roadmap — 53

Chapter 5   Board Materials   81
   Most Requested Board Documents   82
   Leveraging LinkedIn   87

Chapter 6   Board Pitch Prep   97
   Presenting Yourself as Board Ready   98
   Pitch Format   100
   Personal Pitch Do's and Don'ts   103

Section III: EXECUTION   107

Chapter 7   Networking Doesn't Have to
                Be Painful   109
   Build the Right Relationships   110
   Board Networking Strategy   113
   Case Study   113
   When to Approach Others   121

Chapter 8   Board Preparation and
                Interview Process   123
   Tracking Board Openings   124
   Board Interview Preparation   125
   Board Research   126
   Board Search Consultants   130
   The Interview Process   131
   Types of Board Interviews   135
   Top Questions to Prepare Answers For   138
   Questions to Ask the Board   145
   Virtual Meetings: Do's and Don'ts   149

Chapter 9 Goal Setting — 151
Define Your Primary Goal   151
Create Motivation   153

Chapter 10 You Get a Board Offer—Now What? — 157
Conflicts Check   157
Board Contract   164
Questions to Ask   166

Chapter 11 The First 90 Days — 169
You Made It—Now the Real Work Begins   169
Onboarding   172
One-on-One Meetings   175

About the Authors — 177

Notes — 179

Index — 181

Foreword

From my earliest days, governance has been a thread running through my life. My journey began at 16, when I joined the board of my high school's Key Club, a service organization that laid the foundation for a lifelong commitment to board work. Since then, I have served as both inside and outside director on the board of over one hundred public, private, and nonprofit organizations. I continue to enjoy board service, and I currently serve on the boards of thirty organizations.

Over the years, I have come to see that serving on a board is much like participating in a team sport. Trust, teamwork, and a shared vision are fundamental. Boardroom dynamics can make or break an organization just as easily as they can a sports team. The best experiences have always depended on people: a strong, trustworthy CEO, a collaborative board chair, and a group of directors aligned in purpose with more focus on humility and teamwork than on ego. Conversely, I have witnessed dysfunction take root when trust breaks down or when drama takes precedence over diligence.

Not every board or job experience is a good fit, and it is important to understand that you need to "Prepare to be Fired." You will be "fired" more than you might imagine when you are young. Sometimes you fire yourself, but you need to be prepared for circumstances not working out as you had planned. There are times when you will be told that you are not a fit, and other times when you reach that conclusion yourself. Over my lengthy career, there have been five times in my business life and four in my personal life where it became clear that I was not the right person for the situation. In some instances, I was told I was no longer the right person; in other situations I made the decision myself.

The way that you "Prepare to be Fired" is to have your "Escape Routes" thought through in advance when you are in a challenging situation.

This book is a guide for those forging a career in board governance. In my experience, three elements are critical for success as a board member.

1. **Technical Competence:** Board service is not suitable for everyone; it requires aligning your expertise with the needs of the organization. It is critical to develop your knowledge of governance and understand the distinct responsibilities of a director.

2. **Personal Attributes:** Punctuality, preparation, respect, curiosity, and a commitment to continuous learning distinguish outstanding directors. Great board members engage fully, ask incisive questions, and always put the organization's interests first.

3. **Networking and Relationships:** Board appointments are often the byproduct of ongoing relationship building. My board career developed by continually letting my network know that I was interested in board service, advising leaders when opportunities arose, and embracing each new challenge with enthusiasm.

Finding your place on a private or nonprofit board often starts informally—advising a CEO, offering support, and then expressing a willingness to engage more formally. This organic process has opened countless doors for me over the years.

Selection of directors for public companies often takes place by hiring an outside board search firm to provide a list of suitable candidates that meet the criteria established by the nominating and governance committee of the board.

I now spend the majority of my time on board service, and the remainder teaching at the University of Chicago Booth School of Business and participating in leadership programs worldwide. My passion for innovation—whether in technology, governance, or business itself—keeps me learning and contributing to emerging trends, from artificial intelligence to cryptocurrencies.

The best directors never stop learning. Bringing fresh insights to the organizations they serve is a core part of a board member's duty. The board governs; the CEO executes. When this distinction is respected, companies, leaders, and stakeholders all benefit.

My own board journey has revealed the true nature of governance—a constant balancing act between oversight and ownership, strategy, and execution. The best boards, I believe, adopt a "noses in, fingers out" philosophy: deeply informed, setting direction, but not micromanaging.

In my board service, I am candid, sometimes controversial, but always motivated by the desire to advance the organizations I serve and improve the lives of those involved. Preparing for board work takes deliberate effort and reflection. Starting with nonprofit boards is an excellent way to learn and build confidence while making a tangible impact.

Naomi Kent, whose work is featured throughout this book, has often sought my advice, and I hope that the stories and case studies she shares will offer you the tools, clarity, and structure you need to embark on, or deepen your own journey in governance. Whether you are new to boards or a seasoned veteran, you will find frameworks and inspiration to prepare you for the evolving challenges of board service.

If I could offer advice to my younger self, beginning on the Key Club board, it would be to read this book. The lessons within would have saved me from many pitfalls and helped me contribute even more meaningfully along the way.

But above all, remember great governance is never about power—it is always about purpose.

Dennis Chookaszian
Retired chairman & CEO, CNA Insurance Companies
Board member of more than 100 public, private, and nonprofit organizations

Preface

In today's ever-evolving corporate landscape, the concept of a board is both ancient and revolutionary. At its core, a board of directors is a collective of strategic minds entrusted with overseeing how an organization navigates towards its vision. This group is more than a mere assembly of experienced professionals; it's a dynamic force that influences an organization's governance, strategy, and success.

But what exactly is a board? To some, it might seem like an exclusive club reserved for the elite. To others, it is an attainable milestone that represents a pinnacle of career achievement and influence. In truth, a board is a unique entity that brings together diverse perspectives, expertise, and leadership to guide an organization through its challenges and opportunities. The board of directors is the governing body of a corporation or other organization, elected by shareholders and/or stakeholders to set strategy, oversee management, and protect their interests. Board members have a fiduciary responsibility and in many cases it is a legal requirement for organizations to have a board of directors.

This book is for anyone who aspires to join a board. It is for those who want to start a "board career" or build on an existing one.

This book is divided into three sections:

1. **Discovery:** Find out if you actually want to be on a board and, if so, which board is right for you.
2. **Preparation:** Prepare yourself to be considered for a board and ensure that you are a viable candidate.
3. **Execution:** Design a strategy to help you achieve your board aspirations.

In *Wanted → A Board Career: The Definitive Playbook for Landing a Board Seat*, we embark on a journey to demystify the boardroom and help you prepare to join a board of directors. We have a unique set of skills and experience for taking you on this journey.

Naomi Kent is a strategic advisor and mentor to senior professionals who want to build a corporate board career. She spent nearly 13 years with BoardEx, the largest private provider of board and senior executive intelligence, where she interacted with consultants and businesses that engage with all types of boards. While at BoardEx, she saw firsthand how boards operate, how individuals build board careers, and how referrals and references are made for board candidates, and she gained a unique insight into the ecosystem of how boards recruit. Naomi is a trusted partner and strategic advisor to C-suite leaders, senior professionals, active board members, and those seeking board seats, and is a motivating force behind positive career change.

Originally from the UK, Naomi has lived in five countries and moved to the US in 2006. She speaks French and Spanish, is a scuba diver and endurance athlete (having competed in two Ironman races and many long-distance swims), and continues to challenge her disciplined personality with regular competitions.

Marlo Lyons is an award-winning, bestselling author, a licensed (and recovering) lawyer, and a globally certified executive coach who has successfully worked in multiple industries and types of companies from start-ups to the Fortune 500. Marlo has also served on the board of directors for a nonprofit in Los Angeles and works as a strategic advisor and executive coach for board directors and C-suite executives and their teams. Her direct experience in legal risk management, crisis communications, human capital strategies, and organizational transformation, combined with her expertise in career transitions, interviewing, and brand positioning, makes her uniquely suited for providing deep insight into how to successfully attain a position on the right board *for you*.

In her spare time, Marlo is part of "The 5am Club" (based on the book by Robin Sharma), starting every morning with exercise followed by meditation in an infrared spa. She is an avid pickleball player and loves nothing more than enjoying time—including competitive Uno matches—with her husband and two teenage daughters.

In the chapters that follow, we will share our experiences and insights gained from years of involvement with boards and board directors.

Through our stories, you will gain a clearer picture of what it means to be a board member and how you can prepare yourself to be selected for this prestigious role. Whether you are an aspiring board member, a seasoned executive looking to expand your influence, or simply curious about the inner workings of boards, this book will provide you with the tools and knowledge you need to be confident and board ready.

Welcome to this comprehensive guide to unlocking the potential within you and illuminating your path to a successful board career!

Introduction

Every week, we receive emails from senior executives asking, "Do you think it's feasible for me to join a board?" But the real question isn't about feasibility—it's about confidence. They should be asking themselves, "Do I have the confidence to be on a board?" You'd be surprised by how many accomplished professionals who have held leadership roles at the highest levels suddenly find themselves questioning whether they are "good enough" to join a board. Why?

The answer isn't the familiar "imposter syndrome," which is the anxiety or self-doubt that results from persistently undervaluing your competence in having achieved success, attributing career accomplishments to luck or other external forces. You reached your high-level position *because* of your expertise and leadership. Yet stepping into a board role presents a unique challenge because it is uncharted territory, even for those accustomed to being at the top of the corporate pyramid.

Being on a board requires a distinct set of skills that even high-level executives haven't honed because it's not about running a company, it's about *governing* one. This transition can be daunting if you don't understand the nuances of being a board member. CEOs and senior executives often excel as strategic and operational leaders but may feel uncertain navigating the oversight, guidance, and collaborative approach required in board service. And for those who have retired but wish to stay active and contribute, the question shifts: Can they still deliver value in a way that is fundamentally different from their prior roles?

In the past, retirement for many high-achieving professionals often meant stepping back completely and filling their days with activities like tennis, golf, or lunching with friends. Not that there's anything wrong with that! But today, many seek board roles as a way to channel their skills and experiences into meaningful work that keeps them engaged and impactful. This shift is part of a broader trend, where board representation has evolved significantly over the past decade.

While men have historically made up the majority of boards, women are increasingly gaining ground. Recent data indicates that women are now represented on 85% of company boards. The presence of ethnic and racial minorities is also on an upward trend, with 30% representation across surveyed boards.[1]

The path to board service is thus open, but confidence and preparation are the keys to success. Understanding how to leverage your experience, reframe your accomplishments in specific board language, and position yourself effectively can make all the difference in securing and thriving in a board role. Whether you're still active in your career or looking to contribute after retirement, knowing how to transition to a board position is crucial. This book is designed to guide you through that journey.

Common Board Career Myths

There is no single direct path to obtaining a board director position. Yet fellow professionals will often share their advice, sometimes based on their own experience, for how to navigate this process. However well-intentioned, their advice can be either incorrect or only relevant to a unique situation. Let's debunk the top five board career myths.

Myth #1: "I've never been on a board, so I don't qualify for one."

Boards seek people with diverse skills and expertise that align with their strategic priorities—previous board tenure is not always required. If you've been a leader, managed budgets, overseen risk, driven growth, or navigated career transformations, you may already have the governance mindset and skills that corporate boards or nonprofits need. Your ability to bring a fresh perspective, ask insightful questions, and contribute to areas like finance, technology, strategy, or operations can make you a valuable addition to any boardroom. Board experience starts with demonstrating your readiness to take on the role, not necessarily having already done it.

Myth #2: "I need a certification to get on a board."

Certifications in areas such as cybersecurity or ESG (Environmental, Social, and Governance) are a great idea for anyone who wants to feel more confident providing guidance on specific board issues. During interviews or conversations, relevant topics will come up, and if you feel like you will benefit from deeper knowledge, then we strongly recommend them. We also recommend them once you are already on a board and start seeing your own skills gap. On their own, however, certifications won't help you obtain a board role. Boards don't ask for a governance certification to join.

Therefore, while they won't hurt if you want to close a knowledge gap, getting certified in various board-level topics doesn't increase your chances of being selected. In fact, we often recommend to clients who have never served on a board to remove such certifications from their bios and resumes as they might emphasize theoretical education over relevant experience, which is what boards are looking for.

Myth #3: "I need to start creating my board bio first."

This is definitely *not* the first step. A lot of people who decide they want to join a board tend to start with creating and writing their board bio. Completing a bio without knowing which boards you are targeting is like starting to write a book but not knowing the audience, topic, or story. It is nearly impossible! But don't worry. This book will help you take all the right steps in the right order to land the right board job.

Myth #4: "I need to meet lots of board members to get onto boards."

While we do recommend that you start spending time with members of the boards you want to join, they are not always the decision-makers when it comes to recruiting new members. Board members need to remain independent, so inviting friends onto the board can be frowned upon. They will, however, share advice and their unique experiences as board members, and these conversations will provide knowledge about board-level topics. We have found that initial contact with a prospective board member is often made by the CEO or board chair (in some cases, this is the same person) when there is a plan to replace or bring on new members.

Myth #5: "I will need to attend lots of networking events."

In Chapter 7, we go into detail about the value of building relationships and discuss how large networking events aren't necessarily a good use of time when it comes to building a board career. Networking events can take up a lot of time and resources and deliver very little return—especially when you find yourself stuck talking to someone for too long. So if you are the socially anxious type, don't worry that this is required because it is not.

Everything you've *heard* about being on a board—the good and the not so good—will either be validated or proven inaccurate in this book. And while certain career "titles" or "types of people" fit certain boards better than others, there is a nonprofit or for-profit board out there for everyone who wants to be on one.

You may understandably be intimidated, and your board aspirations may feel too big, but this book will alleviate those fears by providing concrete steps toward board readiness so you will feel confident in your pursuit of a board career that is right for you.

Section I

DISCOVERY

CHAPTER 1

Why Join a Board?

"Serving on a board can extend your understanding of your own business because you gain different perspectives, and you meet very interesting people."

—Kerry Moynihan, executive search,
board practice, Boyden

While it would be wonderful if everyone offered to join a board out of pure altruism, the decision to pursue board service is often far more intentional. Even retirees who choose to serve on boards are looking for something deeper than simply filling time or finding a new routine. Joining a board is a significant commitment that requires clarity about your motivations, values, and the impact you hope to make. For some, it's about leaving a legacy or sharing their expertise; for others, it's about professional development, expanding their network, or contributing to a cause or organization they're passionate about. Whatever your reasons may be, taking the time to reflect on what drives you and exploring how board service aligns with your values will help you determine if a particular path is the right fit. Without such self-reflection, you risk pursuing a role that doesn't fit, leaving you feeling dejected.

> **Tip #1: It's not just about being impressive; it's about being aligned.**

Determine Your Motivation

Most board directors have personal motivations for joining a board, and because everyone's reasoning may vary, it's important to clearly identify *your* motivation. There isn't necessarily a "right" motivation, but the most effective board members typically have a combination of motivations that align the organization's mission with their own desire to contribute.

In a proprietary survey we conducted with prospective clients, we asked them to identify their main motivation for joining a corporate board. Following are their top five reasons (they could choose more than one answer, so the results exceed 100%):

79%—To share their expertise with others

63%—To have purpose in their life

53%—To get paid for advisory work (instead of giving advice for free)

47%—As part of their retirement plan to be active and engaged in business

47%—To add to their existing portfolio career (the pursuit of multiple income streams and creative pursuits rather than reliance on a single job)

Understanding your "why" will not only help you identify the right board opportunities but also ensure that your expectations align with the realities of board service. Here are some of the most common motivations and considerations:

1. Making an impact: Many individuals join a board to help shape the direction of an organization, influence policy, or contribute to social causes. Having a passion for the organization's mission and wanting to contribute meaningfully is often key to board effectiveness. And while claiming you "want to make an impact" may sound noble, it doesn't explain the entire motivation. Determine what *kind* of impact you want to make. Do you want to influence the growth trajectory of the company? Will being on the board of a particular organization help broaden your impact in your community? Do you want to make an impact on others on the board and the executive leadership team? Defining your goals will help you be clear on what "making an impact" means so you can determine which board opportunities will potentially be the best fit.

2. Giving back: Many people are motivated by a desire to give back to their community, industry, or an organization they believe in, but simply volunteering is not as appealing as serving on a board. For those who have built successful careers, serving on a board offers a meaningful way to contribute their expertise, time, and resources. Whether it's supporting a community, advancing an industry, or guiding an organization with a mission they believe in, this sense of purpose drives board members to want to make a tangible difference. Giving back is particularly significant in nonprofit or mission-driven organizations, where board members can help shape the direction of critical social, environmental, or educational initiatives, both in their communities and beyond. This altruistic motivation often leads to deep engagement, as individuals are not only invested in the success of the organization but also in its broader impact. Ultimately, the desire to give back can lead to highly fulfilling board experiences, fostering a sense of contribution beyond personal or financial gain. It's important to be aware that many people assume that the words "giving back" reflect an interest in a nonprofit or community-based organization. If you are looking for a paid position on a for-profit company board, you may want to adjust the language you are using when talking about your board interest.

3. Legacy building: For senior leaders and C-suite executives, joining a board is often about expanding an already impressive legacy. After decades of driving growth, innovation, and transformation, the opportunity to serve on a board allows them to extend their impact beyond their own organizations. Board service provides a platform to influence industries, shape future leaders, and contribute to causes or companies that align with their values. By guiding sustainable strategies, fostering strong governance, and ensuring long-term success for organizations that matter to them, it's about leaving a lasting mark beyond personal achievements. For many, it's a chance to shift from building their own legacy to helping others build theirs.

4. Learning and personal growth: Some individuals seeking board positions are strongly motivated by personal growth and the chance to learn. Many professionals view serving on a board as an opportunity to broaden their knowledge and business acumen, particularly in areas like corporate governance, strategic decision-making, and financial oversight. Navigating the complex challenges of an organization from a board perspective can also sharpen problem-solving and crisis management skills beyond functional expertise.

Further, board roles often provide exposure to new industries or sectors, allowing members to gain insights they wouldn't have had in their primary careers. This diverse experience can enhance their leadership abilities, foster critical thinking, and deepen their understanding of complex organizational dynamics. Since boards oversee an entire company, serving on a board will provide a broad understanding of how all the divisions of a company interact. Additionally, the collaborative nature of board work, where members engage with peers from different backgrounds, provides an enriching environment for exchanging ideas and gaining fresh perspectives. For those who value continuous development, serving on a board can be an invaluable learning experience that complements their career while opening doors to new opportunities.

5. Relevance and purpose: A board position can be an attractive option for executives nearing retirement or in retirement to restore a sense of relevance and renewed purpose. Transitioning from a prominent corporate position or entrepreneurship to playing golf or going to lunches with friends can be a difficult shift for business leaders. Joining a board allows senior executives and retired leaders to leverage their extensive experience and insights in a high-level advisory role without the intense time commitment of a full-time job. It provides a fulfilling way to remain active in their industry or explore new sectors while transitioning into a more flexible and balanced lifestyle. At the same time, a board role allows retirees to stay engaged in meaningful discussions, contributing valuable insights and experience in a significant and impactful way without the daily responsibilities of running a company.

6. Connections: Board membership offers a unique opportunity to network with a diverse group of accomplished individuals, including executives, industry leaders, and experts from various fields, in an active and intimate setting. That is why creating new connections is a compelling motivator for many professionals seeking board positions. These relationships can lead to valuable career opportunities, partnerships, or collaborations that might not otherwise have presented themselves. Being part of a board also provides visibility and can strengthen one's reputation within influential circles. However, members who are solely focused on making personal connections without a commitment to the organization's mission or goals risk being perceived as self-serving, thus undermining their reputation. Effective board members contribute to discussions, offer strategic insights, and collaborate with others, building not only professional relationships but also a reputation as a valuable and engaged participant.

7. Influence and power: Influence and power can be enticing motivators as board positions provide a platform to shape high-level decisions and steer the direction of an organization. The ability to contribute to major strategic choices and have a say in governance often attracts those who are drawn to leadership and authority. Seeking a board role solely for the sake of power can, however, be problematic if not coupled with a strong sense of responsibility and accountability. A desire for influence without a commitment to the organization's mission and long-term success can result in decisions that prioritize personal gain over the best interests of the organization.

In addition, approaching a board position from a position of influence and power is unlikely to resonate with chairs or nomination committees responsible for board appointments. These decision-makers are adept at identifying candidates whose primary motivation is personal power rather than contributing meaningfully to the board's work. Candidates who exhibit an eagerness for influence without demonstrating an authentic interest in the organization's goals, values, or challenges will likely be passed over. Successful board members understand that their influence should be used responsibly with a focus on fostering organizational success rather than personal advantage.

8. Status, prestige, and credibility: Some people seeking board membership are motivated by the allure of status and prestige or the potential for enhanced credibility. They enjoy talking about their board work on the golf course or at a dinner party. Serving as a board member can certainly enhance one's professional reputation, signaling leadership, influence, and expertise within their field or industry. Others may see a board director title as a means to establish stronger credibility in a certain sector or confer an authority for speaking engagements. The role itself does carry an inherent level of respect, as it reflects trust and recognition by peers or stakeholders. However, those motivated solely by status may find themselves disengaged from the actual work, leading to underperformance. This not only diminishes the value they bring but can also harm the organization. To truly excel, individuals must pair their desire for prestige and status with a genuine interest in contributing to the board's goals and the organization's success.

9. Travel: Some individuals may be attracted to joining a board because of the opportunity to travel, as many boards hold annual retreats or meetings in desirable locations such as Paris, Tokyo, New York, or London. These gatherings can provide a break from routine and a chance to visit new cities or even countries, providing exposure to new cultures, business practices, and networks. However, travel should not be a primary motivator for seeking a board position. While the idea of attending meetings in exotic places may seem appealing, the reality is that these trips are often limited to just a few times a year and are primarily focused on board business. During these meetings, board members are typically engaged in intense discussions, strategic planning, and critical decision-making, leaving little time for sightseeing or leisure activities. Additionally, travel is often to the organization's headquarters, which may not be a glamorous destination. Ultimately, while occasional travel is a perk, joining a board requires a commitment to the responsibilities at hand. Viewing it primarily as a tourism opportunity will lead to disappointment.

10. Tax advantages: Many *nonprofit* boards expect members to make a personal donation or help with fundraising as part of their board service. This practice is primarily tied to the board's role in governance and supporting the mission. While a personal financial contribution signals a board member's commitment, it can also mean a tax break if the donation is substantial.

11. Compensation: Who doesn't want to get paid for sharing their expertise? Compensation is often a motivating factor for those seeking board positions, especially as that benefit can be significant in certain organizations. Many boards, particularly those in for-profit sectors, provide various forms of financial compensation to their board directors. This often includes retainers (fixed annual fees for attending board meetings) and meeting fees, which are payments for each meeting attended. In addition, some boards offer annual compensation packages that may include cash payments or other benefits. Lodestone Global tracks private company board compensation every year through sector surveys. At least one such survey revealed total median board compensation of $50,400, up 2.4% from 2023.[1] Board members in the financial services sector saw the largest growth in pay with an increase of 6% between 2023 and 2024. Note, though, that some of that compensation may be in equity, not cash.

For corporate for-profit boards, including start-ups, equity compensation is common; this involves granting shares or stock options, which can potentially yield substantial long-term financial gains as the company grows or is acquired. Equity compensation aligns board members' interests with the company's performance, as the value of their shares can increase with the company's success. This financial reward can be significant, providing board members with the potential for considerable earnings beyond their initial compensation. Some early-stage companies also ensure that board members have "skin in the game" by suggesting a minimum personal investment.

For those who have spent years building functional expertise and leadership experience, the financial rewards of serving on a board may seem like a natural progression. However, board positions often require a significant investment of time, energy, and strategic insight; those motivated purely by financial gain may find themselves dissatisfied when faced with the complexities and challenges of the job. Further, nomination committees can tell if money is a driving force behind board interest.

Naomi recalls a client who interviewed for a board of director position with a private company in Tennessee (he lived in Chicago). He had just completed the final round of interviews and was told he should expect a formal offer within a few days. When he arrived at the airport for his trip back home, his flight was delayed for hours due to a winter storm in Chicago. He was so eager to return that he found a flight on another airline, but only a first-class ticket was available. He paid for it and then submitted the $2,500 bill to the nomination committee for reimbursement. That one act sank his candidacy. The board decided that his values were not aligned with the company's values to "spend money like it's your own." Even their executive leadership team doesn't fly first class unless it's an international flight. While this wasn't technically a conversation about board compensation, his behavior was interpreted as reckless, disqualifying him from consideration.

Identify and Define Your Values

If you aren't sure of your motivations, understanding what is important to you will help you consider whether a board position aligns with your values. If your values are fulfilled, you will be fulfilled.[2] So your values hold the key to whether a board career is in your future and whether you will be successful. Remember, being on a board can be a lot of work! The last thing you want to do is join a board of directors and then not enjoy the work because it doesn't align with your values.

To clarify your values, ask yourself the following four questions through a board director lens:

1. What do I like doing or what gives me energy?
2. What do I hate doing or what depletes my energy?
3. In what kind of environment do I thrive and feel most at ease?
4. What kind of interactions do I enjoy and want to have with others?

For example:

What I Like / Gives Me Energy	Corresponding Value
Contributing and feeling valued for doing so	Impact
Learning new things	Learning
Emerging technology	Innovation
Working with authentic, real people	Authenticity
Interacting with smart people	Intellectual challenge
What I Dislike	**Corresponding Value**
Lack of transparency	Transparency/Integrity
Never seeing progress	Growth
When decisions are constantly delayed	Decisiveness
Excessive arguing, not listening	Respect
Back-channeling	Transparency

If, after answering the four questions, you still have trouble identifying the values that align with your answers, try the following prompt in several AI programs such as ChatGPT or Gemini: "What is the corresponding value for [in the case of this example] contributing and feeling valued for my work?" The program will respond with several potential values. If they don't feel right, try a few more times or with different AI platforms, and don't settle for initial responses. Dig deep to understand if a proposed value resonates with you.

Once you have your list of values, create "value strings." Use a stream of consciousness (unedited brainstorming) approach to write down what comes to mind about each value with a slash between each thought. Value strings don't have to be complete sentences. You aren't striving for perfection here. You are simply defining what the value means to you with either words or examples. Here are a few value strings from the above values:

→ **Impact:** Wanting people to feel like I'm contributing / Wanting to know my contributions are valuable / Feeling like the company's direction is more solid because of what I contribute / Knowing that what we do is helping the company be successful / I have a lot of knowledge about different types of companies and I want to share that information / I can see a real difference in a company's trajectory from my contribution

→ **Innovation:** I love learning about new technology and inventions / Technology runs our world, our offices, our lives and I can't learn about it fast enough / Every time something new comes out, I want to dig in and learn about how it works and what it can be used for / I love to innovate something from white space and figure out what can be done with it / I want others to feel passionate about the next big thing like I do / Innovation is my middle name

→ **Authenticity:** I'm a real, no BS type of person and need to connect with other real people / I have never kissed ass to climb a ladder and I don't want to do that on a board / I want to work around people who know who they are, what they want, and how to achieve it in an authentic and honest way / Being around fake people or people who are trying to be something they are not drains me / Let's be direct, tell each other what we think, then make decisions based on fact, data, and relevant qualitative information / Let's not waste time

- **Intellectual challenge:** I must be challenged and engaged in my work / I need stimulating and dynamic conversations or I lose interest / Whether it's problem solving, learning about a budget, why money is spent a certain way, or just learning something new, I need engagement to stay focused / I don't need people to entertain me because that is different than engagement / I need something intellectually stimulating to feel fulfilled and attentive to the discussion / Even a budget can be interesting if you dig into it

- **Growth:** I like to see tangible results, continuous improvement, and forward movement in tasks and projects / Growth doesn't have to be fast, but I have to see some progress toward a shared goal or vision / Sometimes that growth is within me / If the company isn't moving but I am learning and growing, that is fine too / I want to see forward movement somewhere in my life whether it's with the company I'm contributing to, my own life, or in my family's growth

- **Respect:** I need to feel respect to give respect / To me, respect is about truly listening to other perspectives that you may not agree with but are willing to spend more than a second thinking about it / I value open and respectful communication where everyone's voice is heard and different opinions are thoughtfully considered / Respect is about collaboration, where listening and understanding are prioritized over dominating or aggressive behavior such as screaming or fist pounding / I want to be with others who appreciate dialogue and try to understand other perspectives while coming to productive outcomes

- **Transparency:** Similar to respect / Open and honest communication where all discussions are conducted in the room and not back channeled later / If you disagree with someone, say it with everyone present, don't go around people's backs later to get support for your position / Conducting conversations and decisions collaboratively and with integrity / A lack of transparency never leads to anything good / When everyone operates with integrity and fully discloses their thoughts and perspectives, you have true accountability and fairness in the decision-making process

Sometimes this stream of consciousness process will lead to more values that will require a new stream of consciousness. Break them out and do the same exercise. Once you have finished all your value strings, distill each one into a definition that most resonates with that value for you. For example, from the above list:

- **Impact** = Feeling like the company's direction is more solid because of what I contribute.
- **Innovation** = Every time something new comes out, I want to dig in and learn about how it works and what it can be used for.
- **Authenticity** = Let's be direct, tell each other what we think, then make decisions based on fact, data, and relevant qualitative information.
- **Intellectual challenge** = I need stimulating and dynamic conversations or I lose interest.
- **Growth** = I want to see forward movement somewhere in my life whether it's with the company I'm contributing to, my own life, or in my family's growth.
- **Respect** = I value open and respectful communication where everyone's voice is heard, and different opinions are thoughtfully considered.
- **Transparency** = Conducting conversations and decisions collaboratively and with integrity.

Understanding your values will help you find a fulfilling board director position; it will also help a board find you as values need to be aligned. And while you are thinking about values, consider whether you'd like to be a board director in a certain industry or size of company or with a public, private, or nonprofit organization. If you don't yet know what you want, or don't even know what those types of boards are, don't worry! We'll help you figure that out in Chapter 3.

Chapter 1 Summary

1. **Determine your motivation:** Understand the key motivators that are driving you to join a board.
2. **Identify and define your values:** Identify and define what is important to you to understand whether a particular board position aligns with your values.

CHAPTER

Who and What Makes a Great Board Member?

"Think about board service as 'service.' It will be enjoyable, but it is really about the value you bring to the company."

—Sandra Helton, public company board member and former CFO

Anyone can make a great board member, but not everyone will make a great board member for every board. That may seem contradictory, but it's not. There are foundational characteristics that make someone a great board member and it all starts with understanding the board member role.

Understand the Board Member Role

Tip #2: Great board members don't just show up; they level up.

The main difference between being a board member and being an employee is that board directors provide strategic thinking, governance, and oversight while employees implement the mission. Simply put, board members are not executing on the strategy; they are risk mitigators, transformation leaders, and growth enablers.

If you have never been on a board, it is difficult to understand what it means to serve on one. To begin, here is a broad overview of board service.

Primary Responsibilities

There are two ways to look at primary responsibilities, core duties, and expectations for board service:

- **Director responsibilities:** Board members are responsible for acting in alignment with the mission of the company and advancing the company's goals. They must attend and actively participate in board meetings. Board members are also responsible for recruiting the CEO and new board members. Most board members will serve on at least one committee as well as work with the board compensation committee to approve the compensation for the CEO (or executive director at a nonprofit) and, at times, other senior executives. They are responsible for organizational governance to ensure that company policies are advancing the mission and that the company is adhering to regulations.

- **Fiduciary responsibilities:** There are three main areas. The first one is centered around "Duty of Care," which is a standard of conduct that requires people to act with a certain level of watchfulness, attention, caution, and prudence similar to what a reasonable person would do in the same circumstances. "Duty of Loyalty" requires directors to act in the best interests of the organization and to prioritize those actions over their own personal interests or any other conflicting interests. The third, "Duty of Obedience," means the board must ensure that the company stays true to its mission and purpose, and is in compliance with laws, regulations, and its own bylaws.

There is so much more to learn about each of these areas. Consider using Google or an AI program (or both!) to explore and understand these responsibilities in more detail—including the specific roles of secretary, treasurer, and chair—and gauge your interest in each of them.

How Boards Make Decisions

Typically, boards have a structured process that may involve discussion and then voting while adhering to governance rules (usually *Robert's Rules of Order*). They usually have an agenda for each meeting and follow *Robert's Rules of Order* (if you aren't familiar with these, we suggest learning about them). They begin by discussing specific topics or issues that require a vote, sometimes accompanied by a presentation. Experts on the board or on committees presenting information may make recommendations, so board members should come prepared to ask questions. Voting and decision-making are most often done by simple majority, but some issues may require a supermajority, such as in the case of major financial decisions. Some boards may even require consensus. If unanimous consent is required, then every board member must agree.

The decision-making process may be different depending on whether the board is corporate, nonprofit, or governmental (e.g., the Board of Education, which oversees education). On all boards, decisions are recorded in the official minutes.

The Board's Role in Risk Management and Oversight

Boards are actively engaged in risk management to safeguard the organization's sustainability and stakeholder interests. Boards will establish "risk governance" based on the company's "risk appetite"—how much risk the company is willing to take. This appetite is embedded in the company strategy as well as the board's policies and governance frameworks. Board members will regularly review risk reports that are provided by both internal and external auditors and consider multiple risk factors including financial, operational, legal, cybersecurity, regulatory, reputational, and strategic. The board will also oversee crisis management and business continuity plans.

Many publicly traded company boards have three committees dedicated to risk management:

1. the "audit committee," which mainly focuses on financial risk, compliance, and internal controls;

2. the "risk committee," which focuses on enterprisewide risk mitigation; and
3. the "governance committee," which ensures ethical and regulatory compliance.

These committees work together as well as with other board members to provide full risk management and oversight. An important note on the role of these committees: They make *recommendations* to the board, not decisions.

The board's role is to review all documentation that provides information in these areas and ask tough questions about risk exposure and mitigation strategies for both perceived and real threats. The board's role is oversight, insight, and foresight, so members need to be thinking ahead. If there is an immediate crisis, such as a cybersecurity breach or a sudden financial downturn, the board's role is to help guide the company through it. Further, the board should always initiate postcrisis reviews to improve risk mitigation strategies and introduce policies that can mitigate emerging risks based on industry trends.

How a Board Contributes to an Organization's Long-Term Strategy

Boards play a critical role in shaping an organization's long-term strategy by providing the aforementioned oversight, insight, and foresight, and by holding organizational leaders accountable to defined outcomes.

Board members actively support the CEO in defining or approving the organization's mission, vision, and core values to guide decision-making. This ensures alignment between the company's strategy and stakeholder interests. Stakeholders can include shareholders (stockholders), employees, customers, and suppliers. The board will also review and approve senior leadership's long-term growth roadmap with an eye on feasibility, sustainability, and a broad view of risks and opportunities. While the board is not responsible for executing a long-term strategic plan, it will monitor that execution and work with senior leadership to make adjustments based on company performance and market trends.

Board members may also evaluate emerging risks such as economic shifts, technological disruptions, and regulatory changes that could lead to innovation or investment in new markets, products, or services. Those evaluations may lead to potential mergers, acquisitions, or major capital investments to optimize the long-term strategic plan.

Finally, board members must regularly assess the CEO's performance in delivering on the strategic objectives, ensuring that performance metrics and benchmarks are being met and that key initiatives align with financial and operational capabilities.

How Board Members Are Expected to Stay Informed

Board members are responsible for keeping up with industry trends, regulatory changes, and emerging risks that could impact the organization. They should engage deeply with management, review internal reports and quarterly and annual updates, and monitor industry trends and the company's performance in light of new information. Further, board members should be aware of key metrics, market positioning, market research, and competitor analysis as well as any disruptions that may impact the organization.

Board members may not get all this information through the board itself, so it's important that they take the initiative to learn through other sources, such as traditional news channels, *Harvard Business Review*, McKinsey reports, Gartner surveys, and industry- and sector-specific reports. Board members are also encouraged to attend trade shows such as the Consumer Electronics Show (CES), investor summits such as the SelectUSA Investor Summit, and industry conferences such as the J. P. Morgan Healthcare Conference for medical and med-tech companies.

Board members can also engage with industry experts such as economists, analysts, and consultants as well as IT and cybersecurity experts to understand more deeply the risks to the organization.

Now, we know what you're thinking: If board members are expected to manage risk and protect the company by taking on such a wide range of tasks, then why do companies fail?

Boards are composed of well-intentioned, experienced professionals, but people make mistakes. When boards don't ask the right questions, make timely decisions, demand transparency, or stay informed, the consequences can be devastating. The Enron case is a stark reminder that even the most sophisticated organizations can falter when board oversight breaks down.

Once a powerhouse in the energy sector, Enron officially imploded in December 2001 under the weight of accounting fraud, ethical lapses, and catastrophic governance failures. The company's leadership employed deceptive accounting practices to hide billions in debt, inflating earnings, and misleading investors. Yet these actions went largely unchecked at the board level. Why? Because the board failed in several key areas: It accepted overly complex financial explanations without adequate scrutiny, lacked independent oversight, and relied too heavily on information provided by management without challenging its accuracy. In other words, the board did not exercise the diligence and critical oversight required to safeguard the company's long-term health.

Enron's downfall not only wiped out shareholder value and employee retirement savings; it also rocked the global financial system and shattered public trust in corporate governance. This crisis became the catalyst for sweeping reforms, most notably the Sarbanes-Oxley Act of 2002, which introduced stricter oversight requirements, enhanced financial disclosures, and greater accountability for boards and executives alike.[1]

Board Member Attributes

An effective board member possesses a potent combination of skills, experience, and personal attributes which sets them apart from the rest:

1. Strategic thinker: Strategic thinking is the ability to consider the big picture, anticipate future challenges and opportunities, and develop a plan to achieve long-term goals. It involves analyzing complex situations, identifying key priorities, and making decisions that align with overarching financial objectives. By focusing on what is most critical and connecting short-term actions to long-term outcomes, strategic thinkers at the board level understand the organization's vision and can translate how that vision should be carried out beyond short-term goals. Simply put, since the role of board members is to anticipate challenges and identify opportunities for growth, they need to be big-picture thinkers who can make connections between concepts and data that may not be readily apparent.

2. Subject matter expertise: Individuals who have specialized knowledge in areas like finance, marketing, technology, risk management, human capital, go-to-market, or industry-specific expertise make exceptional board members. They bring unique perspectives that complement existing board skills and sometimes facilitate strategic relationships that the company can leverage.

3. Strong governance knowledge: Individuals who are familiar with fiduciary responsibilities, governance best practices, and regulatory compliance have a distinct advantage when being considered for a board position.[2] There is a big difference between governing, which focuses on oversight and strategy, and managing, which handles operational tasks. Most leaders had operational roles prior to joining a board, so being exposed to governance, or working in a governance capacity, makes for an easier transition to board membership.

4. Collaborative and diplomatic: Effective board members thrive in group settings, demonstrating an ability to actively listen, engage respectfully, and consider diverse perspectives. Collaboration requires more than just teamwork, though; it's about fostering an environment where differing viewpoints are valued and contribute to informed decision-making. Diplomacy is equally critical, as it allows board members to navigate complex discussions with tact and professionalism. Balancing assertiveness with a willingness to compromise is essential, ensuring that personal opinions don't overshadow the broader mission and priorities of the organization. This skill set builds trust and drives collective success.

5. Integrity and ethical leadership: Exceptional board members uphold the highest ethical standards, serving as role models of integrity within the organization. They consistently ensure that the organization's actions align with its core values and mission, fostering trust among stakeholders. Ethical leadership requires transparency, accountability, and honesty, even when faced with difficult or complex challenges and decisions. By prioritizing what is right over what is easy or what will keep you on the board protects the organization's reputation and long-term sustainability while demonstrating a commitment to principled governance.

6. Commitment and engagement: The length of board terms varies depending on the type of organization and its governance structure. Some terms are only a year and others may be up to five years or longer. Once elected to a board, you are expected to be committed and engaged throughout the duration of the term. This is why it's important to know whether a board you are interested in has a specific commitment, such as staggered terms or term limits, and what its re-election policies are so you can decide whether you can be fully committed and engaged during your term or beyond.

Board commitment goes far beyond just showing up to meetings. A truly effective board member is deeply invested in the organization's success, actively participates in discussions, and serves as a trusted advisor to leadership. This requires intellectual engagement and strategic thinking regarding the mission, risks, and competitive landscape of the organization. It also requires a commitment to actively building relationships with the CEO, executives, the chair, and fellow board members, and a willingness to step outside the boardroom and connect with employees, customers, investors, or donors to understand broader perspectives that could impact board decision-making.

All this commitment and engagement can take time, an issue that we explore in detail later in this chapter.

7. Effective communicator: Strong communication skills are a cornerstone of board effectiveness. Exceptional board members can clearly articulate their ideas, ensuring that complex concepts are conveyed in a concise and accessible manner. They provide constructive feedback that drives improvement while fostering a collaborative and respectful tone. Effective communicators also excel at asking tough, insightful questions that challenge assumptions and promote deeper discussions, all while maintaining a positive, solutions-oriented approach. Equally important is their ability to actively listen, creating space for diverse perspectives and strengthening group decision-making skills.

8. Visionary yet practical: Outstanding board members possess the ability to balance an inspiring long-term vision with the pragmatism needed to implement realistic, actionable strategies. They focus on guiding the organization toward ambitious goals while ensuring that decisions are grounded in current resources, capabilities, and constraints. By aligning visionary thinking with practical execution, they help create sustainable outcomes that serve the best interests of all stakeholders. This dual perspective ensures that innovation and strategy are both aspirational and achievable.

9. Independent and curious: An exceptional board member brings fresh ideas and perspectives, with a willingness to constructively challenge assumptions when necessary. Independence of thought ensures that decisions are well-rounded, free from groupthink, and focused on the organization's best interests. Coupled with this is an innate curiosity, which is a hallmark of lifelong learners who are eager to explore emerging trends, issues, and technologies that are shaping the future. As Dennis Chookazsian, former CEO and chairman of CNA Financial and current board director on multiple boards, advises, "Noses in, fingers out." It is a well-known caution and essential reminder to ask questions and be continually curious but not get directly involved in the business itself.

10. Passionate advocate: A great board member demonstrates a deep, authentic commitment to the organization's mission and goals. Their passion translates into active engagement, using their network, expertise, and influence to advance the organization's impact. Whether supporting fundraising initiatives, building strategic partnerships, or championing advocacy efforts, they leverage their connections and credibility to open doors and create opportunities. This dedication inspires others and reinforces the board's collective ability to drive meaningful change and support the company's long-term goals.

Do you need to have all the attributes listed above in order to join a board? No! Most executives who are ready to join a board do have many of these attributes, capabilities, and interests, but this chapter is about what makes a *great* board member—something to aspire to. Just know that the best board members not only bring valuable expertise but also align with the organization's culture, values, and long-term objectives.

Time Commitment

As discussed above, the time commitment required by board members might extend far beyond the actual boardroom. At a minimum, board time (board meetings and preparation) will take up roughly 20–60 hours per year. However, when companies are experiencing exceptional circumstances that require additional board commitment, the demand can go way up. According to a "Boards Balance Innovation and Risk" survey by BDO, board members of corporations (not nonprofits) reported that they invest an average of 285 hours a year on their most challenging boards. That's 35 days a year based on an eight-hour workday. Additional surveys of larger boards show median board obligations of 65 direct hours and another 200 hours per year in preparation and research!

When in board meetings, members must be active listeners who are fully engaged in the conversation, committed to being present when called upon, and prepared with questions to help surface relevant information for decision-making. In addition to board meetings and preparation, there may be committee meetings, reviewing internal and external reports, and independent research on market trends. Travel may be required, such as for day-long or week-long meetings, depending on the type of board and its responsibilities. Further, board members may be asked to engage with company personnel outside the boardroom, interview executives for top company leadership roles, and communicate with third party providers as well as investors or shareholders. None of this takes place *in* the boardroom!

The point is that being on a board can be unexpectedly time-consuming, so we recommend that you find out what the required level of involvement will be before you join a board.

Chapter 2 Summary

1. **A board member's role:** Knowing the roles, responsibilities, and core duties of board membership will help clarify expectations for board service.
2. **Board member attributes:** A great board member possesses a combination of skills, experience, and personal attributes that allows them to contribute effectively and sets them apart from those who may not be right for board service.
3. **Time commitment:** Assess whether you have the time to be on a board because it takes commitment and full engagement to effectively contribute to a board's mission.

CHAPTER

Which Board Is Right for You?

"There is no sadder sight than a perfectly good director squandering their skills and experience on the wrong board. It can ruin an otherwise promising career."

—Julie Garland McLellan, board director, CEO, *The Director's Dilemma*

For anyone looking to join a corporate or nonprofit board, remember that having a clear vision of the type of board you are looking for increases your chances of success. We often compare the journey of someone who says, "I would like to join a board," to someone who says, "I am looking for a job." What industry? What field? What specific job? When looking for a job, you can't just say you want to work in HR because many arms of HR exist: HR operations, HR business partner, HR employee relations, HR learning and development, HR program management, the list goes on. The same for boards. Knowing exactly what kind of board you want to join is critical to landing the right board role, because once you know the kind of board you want to join, you can then determine the *value* you can bring to that specific board.

> **Tip #3: Not every board will be right for you, and that's the importance of choosing wisely.**

Types of Boards

First, let's do a quick review of the different types of boards so you understand how to think about which one may be best for you.

Corporate Boards

Corporate boards oversee the governance and strategic direction of for-profit companies, ensuring that the organization fulfills its fiduciary duties to shareholders. These boards often include a mix of internal executives (such as the CEO) and independent directors who provide external perspectives. Their responsibilities include approving major decisions, setting strategic priorities, evaluating the CEO, and ensuring compliance with legal and ethical standards. Corporate boards focus on driving profitability, managing risks, and creating long-term value for stakeholders.

There are two types of corporate boards:

- **Public company boards:** These boards govern organizations whose shares are traded on public stock exchanges such as the New York Stock Exchange or Nasdaq. They have a heightened level of responsibility due to their accountability to shareholders, regulatory bodies, and the broader public. Their primary role is to elect the CEO, provide oversight, approve strategic direction, and make sure that the company is in compliance with legal and ethical standards. Key responsibilities of public company boards include approving major financial decisions such as mergers and acquisitions, declaring dividends, and overseeing the annual budget. They are also tasked with hiring, evaluating, and, if necessary, replacing the CEO to ensure effective leadership. In addition, these boards focus on risk management, protecting the company's reputation, operations, or market position from potential threats.

    Public company boards often include a mix of company executives and independent directors who bring unbiased perspectives and expertise. For example, the board of a company in a global manufacturing business may want to include one or two representatives from different countries where they manufacture or sell their products. Creating such an influential and diverse group of experts will benefit the company's future by maintaining a balance between management insight and external accountability. The stakes for public company boards are high, as their decisions can significantly impact stock prices, market perception, and the company's long-term success. As a result, these boards often operate under intense scrutiny and must be transparent and effective in fulfilling their duties.

→ **Private company boards:** These boards govern privately held organizations, ranging from family-owned businesses to private equity-backed firms. They often focus on CEO development, growth strategies, succession planning, and investment returns for owners. While they don't face the same regulatory scrutiny as public companies, private company boards still uphold fiduciary responsibilities and work closely with management to achieve long-term goals.

Nonprofit Boards

Nonprofit boards focus on advancing the mission of their organization while ensuring financial sustainability and compliance with regulations. Unlike corporate boards, their primary objective isn't profit generation, but delivering on social, cultural, or community goals. Nonprofit board members are often passionate advocates who contribute their time, expertise, and resources to help the organization succeed. Their duties include fundraising, hiring and evaluating the executive director, and ensuring that the organization's activities align with its mission and values.

Nonprofits boards cover a wide range of needed skills and mission-driven outcomes. Finding the right one for you could create an opportunity for your career or waste your time and resources. Here are three questions to ask yourself before seeking out a nonprofit board:

1. Do I connect with its mission/cause? If you are passionate about its mission, you will want to donate your time and money and the experience will be a lot more enjoyable.

2. Is the mission/cause "on-brand"? As in, does the nonprofit line up with your personal brand, other career goals, and/or your future?

3. Will I resonate with current board members? Find out who is on the board. If you won't be engaging with impressive people, don't join that board! You may become frustrated by their lack of experience, potentially having to mentor everyone else, and your networking opportunities will be limited.

Here are some of the different types of nonprofits you may want to consider:

- **Charity:** A charity aims to serve the public interest or common good. Charities typically focus on various purposes, such as:
  - preventing or relieving poverty.
  - advancing education, health, and religion.
  - promoting arts, culture, heritage, or research/science.
  - supporting community development.
  - protecting children, human rights, and animal rights.
  - preserving, restoring the environment.

- **Industry or professional association:** This is a group that serves to advance individuals from the same industry or who are in the same profession (e.g., The American Academy of Ophthalmology). They usually do the following:
  - Support the interests of people working in that profession.
  - Facilitate innovation, communication, and connection.
  - Offer networking opportunities through events and conferences.
  - Provide educational resources or certifications.

- Advocate on behalf of their members and the industry they represent.
- Set industry standards, ethics, and best practices.
- Influence legislation and regulations that impact their profession.
- Offer corporate or individual sponsorship of membership fees.

→ **Professional network or club:** A professional "network" connects individuals around a particular interest, industry, mission, or location (e.g., Young Presidents' Organization—YPO). A professional "club" (e.g., Rotary Club) gives members the chance to build authentic relationships and connections with like-minded, purpose-driven individuals who may not come from the same industry or experience. They both do the following:

- Bring people together who have a common interest.
- Create exclusive events at bars, hotels, gyms, and elsewhere to provide professional and social opportunities.
- Have membership fees.

→ **Foundation:** This is a type of charitable organization that provides funding and support to other organizations or individuals for charitable purposes, primarily through grants. Here are some characteristics:

- It decides where to allocate its funds.
- It has considerable interest in making good investments so it can continue to fund mission-driven causes.
- It raises funds through donations, grants, or investments.
- Foundations may be owned by corporations, individuals, or families.

Corporate Advisory Boards

Corporate advisory boards serve as groups of experts who provide guidance, insights, and industry knowledge to an organization's leadership team. Unlike governing boards, advisory boards don't have fiduciary duties but act as a sounding board for strategic ideas. Organizations often use advisory boards to gain specific expertise in areas like technology, marketing, or international expansion. These boards are especially common in early-stage companies, where founders seek external advice without the formalities of a fiduciary board. However, you will also see a number of large public companies with advisory boards; a good example of this are the scientific advisory boards used by the pharmaceutical industry that are made up of independent scientists.

Public Sector Boards

Public sector boards operate within government agencies or publicly funded organizations such as health authorities or municipal planning committees. Their purpose is to ensure that these taxpayer-funded institutions are run efficiently and in the public's best interest. Public sector boards focus on transparency, accountability, and aligning their decisions with public policy goals. These boards must navigate complex stakeholder dynamics and often balance competing interests while adhering to legal mandates.

Start-Up Corporate Boards

Start-up boards are unique in their fast-paced, dynamic nature, usually consisting of founders, investors, and key advisors. These boards are deeply involved in strategic decision-making, investor funding, and scaling the business. They provide critical guidance to founders while balancing the interests of diverse stakeholders including venture capitalists and early-stage employees who may be shareholders. Start-up boards play a vital role in steering the company through rapid growth and market challenges.

Academic and Research Boards

These boards oversee institutions that are focused on education, science, and innovation. They help advance knowledge, support faculty or research staff, and ensure proper use of funding. They also address the ethical considerations of an institution's work, particularly research involving human subjects or intellectual property. Board members are often drawn from academia, industry, or philanthropy, bringing diverse perspectives to guide the mission. While these are mainly nonprofit boards, they can also be advisory boards.

Fund Boards

Mutual fund boards are a specialized type of governing body responsible for overseeing the operations of mutual funds on behalf of their investors. These boards are unique in the governance and legal landscape because they focus on protecting the interests of individual shareholders who entrust their money to professional fund managers. Mutual fund boards make sure that funds are managed ethically, efficiently, and in alignment with investment laws and objectives. The board's primary responsibilities include monitoring the performance of the fund, evaluating the fees charged by the fund's advisor, and complying with regulatory standards established by entities such as the Securities and Exchange Commission (SEC). They play a crucial role in reviewing the fund's contracts with advisors and service providers, ensuring these agreements serve the best interests of shareholders.

Mutual fund boards emphasize fiduciary duties and legal regulation. They also require a high level of investment or financial experience. The majority of board members are typically independent directors to ensure unbiased oversight. They assess the fund's operations, costs, and performance against benchmarks and peers to ensure fair treatment for investors.

Mutual fund boards operate in a highly regulated environment, given their fiduciary obligation to individual investors. They are a critical safeguard, providing checks and balances to prevent conflicts of interest between fund managers and shareholders. This governance model helps maintain trust and confidence in the mutual fund industry, which is foundational to the broader financial system.

A credit fund is an investment vehicle that holds assets related to credit instruments. Its board of directors oversees the conduct of the institution's business, selects and retains competent management, establishes business objectives, and adopts operating policies to achieve these objectives in a legal and sound manner. These boards also require a high level of financial acumen.

Making Your Board Choice

Deciding which board opportunity is the best fit involves evaluating the alignment between your values, goals, and expertise and the board's mission and expectations. Not all boards are created equal, and this means that the purpose of a board differs from company to company.

Step 1: Aligning Board Type to Your Values

Based on the descriptions above and any further research you have conducted on specific kinds of boards, consider how your values align with each board type. The goal is to find the right fit for both you and the company, otherwise you won't be fulfilled, which could lead to a lack of commitment and engagement and the company not getting what it needs. Here are some ways to analyze your values and how they align to certain types of boards:

- **Community and service-oriented values:** If you are passionate about helping people and making a direct, positive impact on communities, a nonprofit board might align best with your values. These boards often focus on social issues, education, healthcare, or other missions that improve society. The reward is often in knowing that your work benefits others rather than your own financial compensation. If you are considering your first board, this may be a good option.

- **Business and financial growth values:** If you are driven by business success, growth, and profit, you might find a private or public company board more in line with your values. These boards offer opportunities to guide the direction of a company, often with a focus on entrepreneurship, scaling, and driving profits. You will find alignment with your values here if you believe in supporting business growth as a means of contributing to the economy or providing employment in your community.

→ **Corporate governance and strategic impact:** If you are motivated by businesses that follow good governance practices and strategic oversight and enjoy being part of a complex organization, a large public company board may suit you. Public boards oversee companies that are accountable to shareholders, and decisions you make can affect markets, industries, and large workforces. Your values might align here if you believe in transparency, corporate governance, or making an impact on a broad scale.

→ **Hybrid values:** Some private and public boards engage in environmental, social and governance (ESG) initiatives, allowing you to combine your interest in helping "causes" with the financial and strategic aspects of business. Similarly, issue-driven nonprofit boards often require the same strategic thinking and governance that public or private boards need, which can appeal to those with a business mindset who also value community impact.

By reflecting on which of these areas resonates most with your core values, whether it's community impact, financial success, strategic leadership, or a combination of more than one, you can be confident that you are considering boards which align with your personal motivations.

Step 2: Assess Your Experience for the Right Board Fit

To fully determine your fit for a board, review the grid on page 42. Notice how the check marks (X or *) show the type of experience desired for each type of board role, but please note that these are not hard and fast rules. In most instances, these are considered baseline—though not exclusive—requirements. For example, if you have been a public company board director, it doesn't mean that you can't be on a mutual fund board.

Use this chart to assess where you have the most experience and how that aligns to a particular board. And don't forget that the size of the profit and loss (P&L) you managed translates into the size of the company board that might be the best fit.

Experience	Public Company Large Cap	Public Company Mid Cap	Public Company Small Cap	Private: PE Backed	Private: ESOP	Private: Family-Owned	Private: Founder-Owned	Mutual or Credit Fund	Start-up	Nonprofit	Advisory Board: Start-up	Advisory Board: Large Public
C-suite Leadership of Public Company	*	*	*						*	X	X	X
SVP or EVP of Public Company	*	*	*						*	X	X	X
C-suite Leadership of Private Company				*	*	*	*		*	X	X	X
SVP, EVP, or Division Head of Private Company				*	*	*	*		*	X	X	X
Leadership of Employee Stock Ownership Plan (ESOP)					*				*	X	X	X
Leadership of Family-Owned						*			*	X	X	X
Private Equity				*			*		*	X	X	X
Chief Investment Officer								*	*	X	X	X
CPA/Financial Expert	*	*	*	*	*	*	*	*	*	X	X	X

Chapter 3 ■ Which Board Is Right for You?

Experience	Public Company Large Cap	Public Company Mid Cap	Public Company Small Cap	Private: PE Backed	Private: ESOP	Private: Family-Owned	Private: Founder-Owned	Mutual or Credit Fund	Start-up	Nonprofit	Advisory Board: Start-up	Advisory Board: Large Public
P&L Responsibility	X	X	X	X	X	X	X	X	X	X	X	X
Financial Acumen	*	*	*	*	*	*	*	*	X	X	X	X
Government Relations	X	X	X	X	X	X	X	X	X	X	X	X
Founded a Business						X	X		X	X	X	
Founded a Business and Sold it				X		X	X		X	X	X	
Previous Corp Board Experience	X	X	X	X	X	X	X	X	X	X	X	X
Current Corp Board Experience	X	X	X	X	X	X	X	X	X	X	X	X
Capital or Fundraising Experience						X	X		X	X	X	

* ***Must*** have experience. This indicates the boards that usually require this type of experience and so, if you have it, you may want to target them.

X ***Good*** to have experience. This indicates that the experience may make your transition onto one of these boards a little easier.

Note: Even if you don't check any of these boxes, consider not-for-profit organizations and advisory board positions where you can share your expertise.

Making Your Board Choice

Now that you know your values and you've dug deep into your relevant experience, check one of the boxes below to indicate what types of boards you will target:

ADVISORY BOARD

☐ Start-up or Early Stage

☐ Public Company

☐ Private Company

☐ Other _____

CORPORATE PUBLIC

☐ Small Cap

☐ Mid Cap

☐ Large Cap

☐ Other _____

CORPORATE PRIVATE

☐ Family Owned

☐ Founder Owned

☐ Private Equity Backed

☐ ESOP

☐ Other _____

FINANCIAL

☐ Mutual/Credit Fund

☐ Credit Union (mostly nonprofit)

☐ Other _____

NONPROFIT

☐ Charity

☐ Industry or Professional Association

☐ Professional Network or Club

☐ Foundation

☐ Other _____

Your Reasons for Choosing Each Board

Be clear about *why* you've chosen to pursue certain boards. Include in your description how your experience and expertise can bring value to these types of boards, and why you are interested in pursuing them based on your values and interests.

_____

_____

_____

_____

_____

_____

_____

Step 3: Find Companies That Align to Your Board Type

Once you've determined the type of board you plan to pursue, the next step is to research specific companies or organizations to target.

There are a range of databases such as BoardEx, Dun & Bradstreet, Director Moves, Zoominfo, Pitchbook, FactSet, and Bloomberg[1] where you can search for specific companies based on your criteria. If you don't want to subscribe to one of these services, consider a simple Google or AI search with prompts such as "What are the top 20 mid-cap companies?" If you know the industry you want to target based on your expertise, try "What mid-cap companies are in the retail space?" If you are looking for struggling companies because you have expertise in turnarounds or restructuring, try "Give me a list of 20 mid-cap companies that are struggling in the economy today."

Research the backgrounds of current board members to understand how the board is structured and whether your skills align with theirs. For example, Naomi worked with a client from wealth management who aspired to join Duolingo's board because of his passion for languages. His research revealed that Duolingo's board prioritized expertise in education policy and e-commerce, not wealth management or interest in speaking languages. While disappointing, this insight saved him time by ruling out a poor fit and narrowing his search toward more suitable boards that aligned with his values and interests.

If you are seeking to join a nonprofit board, identify leaders in your industry or field of work and which boards they sit on. You can also look for nonprofits that align with your career goals. Be sure to review the board of directors of any nonprofit you plan to contact before moving ahead, and consider volunteering before reaching for a board seat. That way they get to know you and you get to know the organization.

Here are some due diligence tips to guide you in your continued research:

- **Confirming values alignment:** Assess whether you genuinely believe in each organization's mission. As we've stated, serving on a board requires more than just a professional commitment; it demands a personal connection to the organization's purpose or product/service. If the organization's mission doesn't resonate with you, you will likely become unfulfilled and disengage from your role over time.

- **Deeper research:** Dive into annual reports, strategic plans, and recent news to understand an organization's performance and direction. Do you agree with the direction? Do you have a different belief of where the organization should grow? Differences don't necessarily mean it's not a good board fit because you may be deriving conclusions from limited research, or you have broader industry knowledge that the board is unaware of.

- **Skills fit and contribution:** Consider whether your skills and experience can add meaningful value. Assess if your expertise fills any gaps or enhances the board's existing capabilities. A well-rounded board benefits from a diverse range of talents and perspectives, so it's essential to identify how you can contribute. To find the right fit, research the specific roles and responsibilities of the boards you're interested in. Look at the backgrounds of current board members. Does your background fit the profile of a typical board member for this company's board? If it's different, how? Will you be adding value to the expertise already on the board or will you need additional years of specific experience?

→ **Time commitment:** As we have made very clear, serving on a board requires a significant time commitment, which can vary depending on the organization. To determine if you have sufficient bandwidth, research the expected time requirements for the boards you're interested in and then try to meet with current board members to find out about meeting frequency, preparation time, committee participation, and additional responsibilities. While the full extent of the commitment may only become clear during the interview process, speaking with individuals in your network who serve on similar boards or have experience in the relevant industry can offer valuable insights into actual time demands.

→ **Financial and legal responsibilities:** Serving on a corporate board of directors or a nonprofit board comes with significant financial and legal responsibilities. Board members are tasked with overseeing the financial health of the organization, ensuring compliance with laws and regulations, and mitigating potential risks. As a fiduciary, you have a legal obligation to act in the best interests of the organization and its stakeholders. Therefore, research the governance regulations that apply to the boards you are considering, and take the time to learn about the specific legal responsibilities of board members. This will help you assess whether you are prepared for these demands and comfortable with the level of accountability required.

→ **Organizational health:** Research each company's financial condition, leadership team, and reputation in the industry. A strong, well-managed organization is more likely to provide a fulfilling and sustainable board experience. Joining the board of an organization in distress can also be rewarding if you're ready for a challenge, but it comes with increased risks. To assess this, conduct thorough research into the company's history, management, clients, and suppliers. Explore platforms like LinkedIn, Glassdoor, and other social media sources to gauge the organization's public image and employee sentiment. For more candid insights, sites like Fishbowl or Reddit can offer anonymous discussions that help you better understand the company's internal dynamics and public perception.

→ **Expectations for raising capital, fundraising, or advocacy:** Many boards, particularly in the nonprofit sector and start-ups, expect members to contribute more than just their time. This may include financial contributions, active fundraising, advocacy efforts, and volunteer requirements. In the case of corporations, especially early-stage companies, the board may be called upon to assist in funding rounds or capital raising for acquisitions. It's crucial to assess whether you're comfortable with these expectations and whether they align with your capacity and willingness to engage. To find out, ask about the organization's fundraising and capital-raising expectations during the interview process. Speak to current or former board members to understand the level of involvement required outside of board meetings. Make sure you are fully aware of these commitments before accepting a position.

Make a checklist or template to help evaluate each specific board opportunity. If the position aligns with your values, skills, and personal goals, it could be a rewarding experience that allows you to make a meaningful impact. If not, it's okay to pass. It's better to wait for the right fit, even if you don't know when the next offer will come through.

Chapter 3 Summary

1. **Align board roles to your values:** Review your values and how they align to different types of boards to gauge the potential for service fulfillment.

2. **Assess your experience for board fit:** Assess where you have the most experience and how that aligns to each type of board.

3. **Find companies that align to your board type:** Research companies where your experience can bring the most value and whose mission and values align with yours.

Section II

PREPARATION

CHAPTER

Preparing Your Brand

"If you are invited to the table, then speak. If you want to be heard at the table, then speak the language of the people who are listening."
—Carla Harris, public company board member and senior client advisor at Morgan Stanley

When you are interviewed for jobs in either the corporate world or nonprofit sector, you probably tailored your resume and LinkedIn profile to match the job description in an effort to sell yourself as the ideal candidate. The overall concept of promoting yourself onto a board is different, however; you need to appeal to the audience more than the organization. Here is a five-step approach to prepare your "brand":

Tip #4: Speaking board-level language will ensure they hear your value.

Brand Roadmap

1. Identify Core Accomplishments

If you are already on a board and are seeking a new or different kind of board, write down your board accomplishments. If you have never been on a board, write down your more significant achievements in the workplace as a leader. Be sure to frame your accomplishments through the lens of being a board member, specifically referencing growth, transformation, and risk.

Growth: When reflecting on your contributions, think about how you helped a business grow in measurable ways. Did you play a key role in expanding into new markets, launching innovative products or services, or driving strategic partnerships? Highlight specific accomplishments that resulted in tangible business expansion, whether through increasing market share, opening new revenue streams, or leading transformational projects. Focus on your ability to identify growth opportunities and foster innovation, showcasing how your leadership directly contributed to the company's development and long-term success. These achievements demonstrate your value as a board director who can bring a growth-oriented mindset to the organizations you serve.

> **Example:** *"During my time as a senior executive at [company name], I led a strategic initiative to expand into new international markets. By identifying key opportunities and strategic partnerships in Asia and Europe, I was able to influence senior leadership to develop tailored products and services that met the specific needs of those markets. I forged partnerships with local distributors and negotiated key agreements that streamlined our entry. This growth strategy increased our market share, positioning the company as a global player in our industry and opening up new long-term revenue streams that exceeded the projected return of 28%."*

Transformation: If you played a key role in helping a company transform, emphasize how you led or influenced those changes. This could involve spearheading a digital initiative that modernized the company's operations, implementing new technologies that improved efficiency, or driving cultural shifts that reshaped the organization's values and employee engagement. If you were involved in mergers and acquisitions, highlight how your leadership helped integrate teams, streamlined processes, or optimized the company's structure for growth. Focus on your ability to manage complex, high-stakes change, navigating challenges while ensuring a smooth transition. Demonstrating your experience in leading transformation shows your capability to adapt, innovate, and strategically guide companies through pivotal transitions.

> **Example:** "At [company name], I led a comprehensive digital initiative that reshaped the company's entire operational model. Facing outdated systems and inefficient processes, I spearheaded the strategy development team and then influenced executive leadership to invest in cutting-edge cloud technology and automated workflows by showing them how the investment would reduce operating costs by at least 15%. Through this process, I also oversaw a major cultural shift, introducing Agile methodologies across teams to foster innovation and collaboration. This transformation enabled the company to adapt more quickly to market changes and become more customer focused. The initiative not only modernized the company's infrastructure and reduced operational costs by 30% over five years, but increased employee engagement by 12% based on our latest engagement survey. All of this positioned [company name] for sustained growth in a highly competitive market."

Risk: Successfully managing risk is a critical aspect of board leadership. In your board experience, focus on how you helped identify, assess, and mitigate potential risks that could impact the organization. These could include financial risks, such as managing debt or investment strategies; operational risks, such as ensuring business continuity through financial crises (or the pandemic); or compliance risks tied to regulatory requirements. Highlight specific examples where your strategic oversight helped the organization avoid or minimize losses, such as navigating a market downturn, cybersecurity threats, or legal challenges. Emphasize your ability to foresee risks and implement proactive measures, demonstrating your expertise in safeguarding the organization's long-term sustainability and success.

> **Example:** "While serving as the CIO of [company name], I played a key role in strengthening the company's cybersecurity strategy. After identifying potential vulnerabilities in our digital infrastructure, I presented to the executive leadership team and the board a comprehensive risk assessment and led efforts to implement stronger security protocols. With full stakeholder alignment, my team prioritized upgrading encryption technologies, improving data breach response plans, and launching companywide cybersecurity training to enhance employee awareness. Additionally, we partnered with external experts to conduct regular security audits and stress tests. As a result, the company was able to prevent several attempted breaches and mitigate the risk of significant financial and reputational damage. Our proactive approach not only safeguarded sensitive data but also positioned the company with our customers as a trusted leader in cybersecurity."

For each accomplishment, think about not only the outcome but also the type of project, the key role you played, and any leadership milestones. Notice how each of the examples above highlights not only personal skills but also the ability to influence change, drive results, and lead during ambiguity.

Don't skip this step! This is critical for your brand positioning, and you will need these accomplishments again in Chapter 8 when we discuss interviewing.

2. Articulate Your Unique Value Proposition

To truly stand out as a serious board candidate, focus on the distinctive expertise or experience that only you can bring to the table. What have you done that few others can claim? Perhaps you've led a company through a significant crisis, such as navigating a cyberattack, or managed a major corporate turnaround under extreme pressure. Have you been involved in M&A (Mergers & Acquisitions) transactions? Maybe you're an expert in emerging technologies like AI or blockchain, bringing cutting-edge insights into industries still adapting to digital transformation. Have you successfully integrated ESG (Environmental, Social, and Governance) policies into a business strategy? Or perhaps you've operated in niche markets that others overlook, like leading the expansion of a business into Africa or South America, giving you unparalleled knowledge of unique cultural and regulatory challenges that the company will face.

Also, think about your fiduciary responsibilities in a new light. For example, have you been responsible for deploying multimillion-dollar investments into developing markets or handling intricate cross-border mergers? Did you mentor the CEO of one of your subsidiary businesses? Your unique experience should be something that adds a new dimension to the board, offering perspectives they haven't had access to before.

> **Example:** *"I bring unique value as someone who led one of the first successful integrations of AI-driven decision-making in a highly regulated industry. At [company name], I pioneered a system that used machine learning to predict and mitigate financial risks, reducing exposure by 20% while staying fully compliant with stringent regulatory requirements. Additionally, having managed operations across six continents, including difficult-to-penetrate markets in Africa, I have a deep understanding of global regulatory landscapes and cultural sensitivities. This combination of technological foresight and broad operational experience uniquely equips me to guide boards looking to innovate while navigating complex social and governance issues."*

3. Master Board-Level Language

Now that you've outlined your accomplishments, it's time to translate them into board-level language. Think of these as the "keywords" you'd tailor for a resume, except in this case, they're essential for positioning yourself across board roles.

Board terminology evolves, just like industry trends. What was once Diversity, Equity, and Inclusion (DEI) has expanded to Diversity, Equity, Inclusion, and Belonging (DEIB). At the time of writing this book, DEIB is being rebranded and redefined again in certain corporations.

Similarly, Corporate Social Responsibility (CSR) transitioned into the broader framework of Environmental, Social, and Governance (ESG). More recently, it is also being referred to as just "Sustainability." Staying current with these shifts is crucial to demonstrating your boardroom readiness.

Your goal is to now refine your accomplishments from Step 1 and your unique value from Step 2, shaping them through the lens of board responsibilities and language. Think of it like speaking to a room full of golfers: You wouldn't want to mix up a birdie with a bogey! The same principle applies here: Mastering board terminology ensures that you can confidently engage in discussions, align your expertise with board priorities, and clearly articulate the value you bring to the table.

Below are the most commonly used board terms along with examples of how they can be used to explain your achievements and accomplishments through a board lens:

Agenda Setting—The process of determining the topics and issues that the board will discuss and act upon in meetings.

> **Example:** *"I ran numerous strategic planning sessions where I led stakeholders in **agenda setting** so those meetings were engaging and productive."*

Audit Committee—Responsible for overseeing financial reporting, internal controls, audit processes, risk, and ensuring compliance with legal and regulatory requirements.

> **Example:** *"In my previous role, I had the opportunity to collaborate closely with the **audit committee** to address some key issues surrounding financial reporting and internal controls. I helped ensure that the company was not only compliant with all regulatory requirements but also took proactive steps to improve transparency and streamline our audit processes. I believe that my experience in working with the **audit committee** will enable me to bring a strategic perspective to any board, ensuring that robust financial oversight is always a priority."*

Change Management—Guiding and supporting an organization through significant transformations to ensure successful adoption of new strategies, systems, or structures while minimizing disruption.

> **Example:** *"When we decided to replace the CMO, who had been with the company for 20 years and was highly respected by everyone, we knew the **change management** process would need to be carefully planned to ensure a smooth transition and maintain morale."*

Compliance—Adhering to laws, regulations and standards, and ethical practices in the board's activities.

> **Example:** *"As a senior leader, I made sure that our company maintained strict **compliance** with industry regulations and federal laws, implementing robust internal controls and overseeing regular audits to mitigate risk and avoid potential legal liabilities. This responsibility has prepared me well for the governance and fiduciary oversight required in a board role."*

Conflict of Interest—Situations where a board member's personal or professional interests may conflict with their duties to a company.

> **Example:** *"In my current role as [title] of an oil and gas firm, there are **no conflicts of interest** preventing me from entering the consumer products market. My expertise in logistics and supply chain means I can provide a different perspective on how companies can grow in this sector."*

Consensus Building—The process of facilitating agreement and alignment among diverse stakeholders by addressing their concerns and finding mutually acceptable solutions.

> *Example:* "In my role as a senior leader, I successfully led **consensus-building** efforts by engaging key stakeholders across departments to develop a unified strategy for a major organizational change. All perspectives were considered, which fostered a collaborative environment that resulted in widespread support and smooth implementation."

Corporate Social Responsibility (CSR)—The board's involvement in ensuring the company acts in a socially responsible manner.

> *Example:* "As a leader on a cross-functional **CSR** committee, I spearheaded the development and implementation of a comprehensive sustainability program that reduced the company's carbon footprint by 30% over three years while also launching community outreach initiatives that supported local education and job training. This work enhanced our reputation for corporate social responsibility and positively impacted both the environment and the communities we serve."

Critical Decision-Making—Making high-stakes decisions under pressure, often with limited information, that significantly impact an organization's strategy, operations, or outcomes.

> *Example:* "As chief human resources officer, I demonstrated **critical decision-making** by swiftly aligning other leaders in a new strategic direction during a market downturn, evaluating various scenarios, and implementing a plan that not only mitigated immediate financial risks but also positioned the company for long-term growth and stability."

Chapter 4 ■ Preparing Your Brand

Crisis Management—The process of preparing for, responding to, and recovering from significant, unexpected events that pose a threat to an organization's operations, reputation, or stakeholders.

> **Example:** *"As chief marketing officer, I effectively managed a major data breach by quickly implementing a **crisis response plan**, coordinating with the IT, legal, and communications teams to address the issue, safeguard sensitive information, and communicate transparently with stakeholders and customers, ultimately minimizing the impact and restoring customer trust."*

Cross-Functional Collaboration—Working effectively with teams from different departments or disciplines to achieve common organizational goals and drive comprehensive solutions.

> **Example:** *"As chief experience officer, I led a successful **cross-functional collaboration** initiative by coordinating efforts between the marketing, product development, and sales teams to launch a new product line. This led to a 25% increase in market share and demonstrated the power of integrated perspectives and teamwork in achieving strategic objectives."*

Cybersecurity Oversight—The board's responsibility to ensure that the company has robust measures in place to protect against cyberthreats.

> **Example:** *"As chief information officer, I provided crucial **cybersecurity oversight** by implementing a multilayered security strategy that includes advanced threat detection systems, regular vulnerability assessments, and comprehensive employee training programs. This has significantly reduced the risk of data breaches and established robust protection for the company's digital assets."*

Enterprise Risk Management (ERM)—The process of planning, organizing, and controlling activities to minimize the effects of risk on a company.

> **Example:** *"One of my greatest accomplishments was implementing an **enterprise risk management** framework that identified and assessed key financial, operational, and strategic risks across the organization while integrating risk management into our strategic planning processes. This included establishing a cross-departmental risk committee which worked to develop effective mitigation strategies and contingency plans, enhancing our ability to respond to potential threats and uncertainties and ultimately strengthening our overall resilience and stability."*

Environmental, Social, and Governance (ESG)—The board's involvement in ensuring that the company acts and reports in a socially responsible manner.

> **Example:** *"As an **Environmental, Social, and Governance** champion, I have had to influence the board's risk appetite for an ESG strategy. Since the board had not approved our new ESG plan, I had to present a proposal on how a strong ESG strategy would not only improve the company's environmental footprint and social impact but also strengthen stakeholder trust and position the company as a leader in responsible corporate practices."*

Ethical Oversight—The board's responsibility to ensure that the company's practices align with ethical standards.

> **Example:** *"As general counsel, I provided **ethical oversight** by leading the development of a robust code of ethics and developing the strategy for conducting regular training sessions for employees on compliance and ethical behavior. As part of this effort, I influenced the company to establish a confidential reporting system for ethical concerns and made sure that all business practices adhered to both legal standards and company values. This effort helped maintain a culture of integrity and transparency while mitigating legal and reputational risks."*

Executive Leadership Team (ELT)—The group of senior executives responsible for setting strategic direction, making high-level decisions, and overseeing the implementation of the organization's goals and policies.

> **Example:** *"As a member of the **executive leadership team**, I collaborated with other senior leaders and the board of directors to develop and execute a strategic plan that repositioned the company in the market, driving a 20% increase in revenue over two years."*

Fiduciary Duty—The legal responsibility of board members to act in the best interest of the company and its shareholders.

> **Example:** *"As general counsel, I continually fulfill my **fiduciary duty** by meticulously overseeing the company's compliance with regulatory requirements and safeguarding the interests of shareholders. I ensure that all legal and financial disclosures are accurate and timely, manage potential legal risks, and provide strategic advice to the board to help them make informed decisions, thereby protecting the company's integrity and maintaining shareholder trust."*

Financial Acumen—The ability to understand and interpret an organization's financial statements, key performance indicators, and overall financial health to make informed decisions on budgeting, capital allocation, risk management, and investment strategies.

> **Example:** *"While I'm the chief marketing officer, I also have strong **financial acumen** regarding the organization's financial sustainability and growth. My goal is to balance both short-term with long-term value creation while also maintaining compliance with financial regulations."*

Financial Oversight—Monitoring and managing an organization's financial performance, ensuring accurate reporting, adherence to financial controls, and alignment with strategic goals.

> **Example:** *"As chief product officer, I provided **financial oversight** by closely monitoring the budget for product development and ensuring that all expenditures were within allocated limits. I collaborated with the finance team to analyze product profitability, assessed return on investment for new initiatives, and made data-driven decisions on resource allocation. By implementing rigorous financial controls and regularly reviewing project costs and revenues, I made sure that product investments were strategically aligned with the company's financial goals and delivered expected value."*

Global Perspective—The ability to consider and integrate international trends, markets, and diverse cultural insights into decision-making by understanding economic, political, tax, and regulatory environments across different regions, as well as recognizing the impact of globalization on an organization's strategy, risks, and opportunities.

> **Example:** *"As the head of product development, I have a **global perspective** that has helped my current company navigate cross-border challenges, expand market reach, and stay competitive in a globalized economy."*

Governance—The system of rules, practices, and processes used by boards to oversee the management of the organization, ensuring accountability, fairness, and transparency in a company's relationship with its stakeholders, including shareholders, employees, customers, and the community.

> **Example:** *"As a member of the executive leadership team, I enhanced **governance** by establishing a formal committee structure to oversee key areas such as compliance, risk management, and strategic initiatives. I*

> *implemented regular ELT meetings and detailed reporting processes, ensuring that all major decisions were made transparently and in alignment with company policies and regulatory requirements. This approach improved accountability, facilitated more informed decision-making, and reinforced a strong governance framework that supported the organization's long-term objectives."*

Human Capital—A general reference to people as related to organizational operations, growth, transformation, and risk.

> **Example:** *"As a senior leader, I view **human capital** as a strategic asset which requires yearly organizational talent planning. I invest in leadership development, employee engagement, and succession planning to drive long-term growth and resilience."*

Influence—The ability to affect, shape, or change the thoughts, behaviors, decisions, or actions of others, often without direct authority, using persuasion, communication, relationships, or expertise to guide people towards a desired outcome.

> **Example:** *"As a business leader, I used my **influence** to encourage the executive team to adopt a more sustainable business strategy. Without direct authority over day-to-day operations, I leveraged my expertise in environmental practices and built strong relationships with key stakeholders, persuading them through data and effective communication to prioritize long-term sustainability over short-term gains, helping to shape a new direction toward responsible growth."*

Innovative Leadership—The ability of a leader to inspire creativity and drive change by fostering an environment that encourages experimentation, forward-thinking, and adaptability.

> **Example:** *"As senior vice president of finance, I actively seek out new opportunities to be an **innovative leader**, which means being open to unconventional solutions that can set us apart from the competition. I am always looking at how every innovation aligns with our long-term vision, so we can drive meaningful transformation while securing sustainable growth."*

Materiality—The significance of an event or of information that could influence the decisions of the board or shareholders.

> **Example:** *"As general counsel, I of course deal regularly with lawsuits, but I only bring those that are **material** to the board such as a patent infringement that could carry a large financial liability, impact the company's reputation, and influence both strategic decisions and shareholders' confidence."*

Mergers and Acquisitions (M&A)—The process of consolidating two or more companies into a single entity, either by merging them or by one company acquiring another.

> **Example:** *"As a senior leader reporting to the executive leadership team, I am always looking for **M&A opportunities** that would be a strategic fit and could expand market share, increase operational efficiency, or gain access to new products, technologies, or markets, contributing to long-term value creation for shareholders while minimizing risk."*

Oversight—Supervisory or advisory role in monitoring key functions that are designed to align operations, processes, and decisions with organizational goals, regulations, and governance standards.

> **Example:** *"My **oversight** of product development means I am providing strategic guidance, assessing risks, and holding the executive team accountable for their decisions and actions. Effective oversight helps safeguard the organization's integrity, ensures transparency, and protects the interests of shareholders and stakeholders by promoting sound governance and ethical practices."*

Profit and Loss (P&L) Responsibility—Accountability for a company's revenues, costs, and expenses, ultimately determining its profitability.

> **Example:** *"In managing the financial performance of the R&D division, I have a $300M **P&L responsibility** which includes budgeting, forecasting, analyzing financial results, and making strategic decisions to maximize profits while minimizing costs in the overall context of the financial health of the company."*

Proxy Statement—A document that provides shareholders (including board members) with information on issues to be voted on at an annual meeting.

> **Example:** *"I am responsible for submitting our company's governance practices, financial performance, and recommendations on proposals in our **proxy statement**."*

Regulatory Knowledge—Specific experience in industries with complex regulatory environments (e.g., financial services, pharmaceuticals).

> **Example:** *"I have **regulatory knowledge** and expertise across a wide range of highly regulated industries and environments including financial services, medical devices, telecommunications, and utilities."*

Risk Appetite—The level of risk a board is willing to accept in pursuit of the company's objectives.

> **Example:** *"In my previous roles, I consistently assessed and aligned the organization's **risk appetite** with our strategic objectives, ensuring that we pursued growth opportunities while effectively managing potential threats to our overall success."*

Risk Management—The process of identifying, assessing, and prioritizing risks that could negatively impact an organization's operations, finances, reputation, or compliance with regulations.

> **Example:** *"While overseeing business services, I worked closely with executive teams to implement comprehensive **risk management** frameworks, ensuring that we proactively identified, assessed, and mitigated key risks while safeguarding the company's assets and aligning with our long-term strategic goals."*

Shareholder Activism—Efforts by shareholders to influence company behavior, often through board actions.

> **Example:** *"Since the bank I worked for is privately owned, I spent a lot of time effectively addressing the concerns of shareholders, recognizing the importance of **shareholder activism** as a catalyst for positive change and a means to enhance corporate governance and accountability."*

Stakeholder Engagement/Alignment—The board's role in ensuring that the interests of shareholders and other stakeholders are considered in decision-making.

> **Example:** *"In all my roles, I have prioritized **stakeholder engagement** by fostering open communication and collaboration, ensuring that the interests of both shareholders and other **stakeholders are aligned** with our strategic decisions for sustainable growth and success."*

Stakeholder Resolutions—Proposals submitted to shareholders for a vote at the company's annual meeting, often addressing governance or social issues.

> **Example:** *"As a nonprofit board member, I have actively reviewed and considered **stakeholder resolutions**, recognizing them as important opportunities to address governance and social issues that reflect the values and expectations of our shareholders and the broader community."*

Strategic Oversight—The board's role in supervising and guiding the strategic direction of the company.

> **Example:** *"I work closely with my team to establish clear objectives and direction, ensuring that our initiatives align with the company's vision and drive long-term success. I then provide **strategic oversight** to keep these initiatives moving in the same direction while introducing and monitoring critical milestones."*

Succession Planning—The process of identifying and preparing future leaders to take over key roles within the company, especially the CEO.

> **Example:** *"I conduct organizational talent planning at least once a year which also includes **succession planning** so we know who is ready to take the helm and what additional development may be needed to prepare them."*

Transformation—A comprehensive change in an organization's structure, culture, processes, or technologies to improve performance, adapt to market dynamics, and enhance competitiveness, which can include implementing new business models, adopting innovative technologies, restructuring teams, or shifting organizational culture.

> **Example:** *"We realized we needed a complete **transformation** to drive growth, respond effectively to internal and external challenges, and reposition the organization for future success."*

If you already serve on a board and are using your board experience to establish your brand, then consider incorporating this additional language into your accomplishments:

Board Committees—Subgroups within the board such as audit, compensation, and nominating committees, focused on specific areas.

Board Evaluation—The assessment of a board's performance and effectiveness, often conducted annually.

> **Example:** *"In my previous role as a board member, I was involved in our annual **board evaluation** process, where we assessed the effectiveness of our board's performance and identified areas for improvement. We gathered feedback from all board members and key stakeholders, analyzed our governance practices, and set clear goals for the upcoming year. This process helped strengthen our decision-making and ensured we were aligned with the organization's evolving needs. I found this exercise invaluable in driving continuous improvement and fostering a more effective, collaborative board environment."*

Board Interlocks—Situations where members of one company's board also serve on another board, potentially influencing decisions or creating a conflict of interest.

> **Example:** *"In my previous board role, I encountered a situation where one of our board members also served on a nonprofit board with a member of a key competitor—an obvious case of **board interlock**. To address this, we established clear boundaries and requested that our board member step off the nonprofit board, which he did. Additionally, we had open conversations about potential conflicts and put in place recusal procedures for any discussions where there might be an overlap of interests. By taking these steps, we were able to maintain transparency and safeguard the integrity of our decision-making process, which ultimately strengthened the trust among board members and the company."*

Board Refreshment—The process of regularly bringing in new board members to ensure fresh perspectives and skills.

> **Example:** *"During my tenure as a board member with [name of company], I was actively involved in a **board refreshment** process where we brought in new members with diverse skills and fresh perspectives after three board members retired. While serving on the nomination committee, I helped identify key areas where we needed additional expertise (such as digital transformation) and assisted in recruiting individuals who could bring valuable insights into these areas."*

Compensation Committee—Oversees and determines the compensation packages for the company's executives, including the CEO and other senior management.

> **Example:** *"During my time on the **compensation committee** at [name of company], I worked alongside fellow board members to evaluate executive compensation structures and ensure alignment with both the company's strategic goals and industry standards. We also focused on enhancing performance metrics to make sure that our decisions were equitable, transparent, and compliant with regulatory guidelines. My role involved providing insights into compensation trends and collaborating with a compensation consultant to implement changes that supported both short-term performance and long-term retention. This experience has deepened my understanding of the responsibilities of board committees and the importance of collaboration in driving organizational success."*

Director Independence—The measure of a board member's ability to make decisions free from external influences or conflicts of interest.

> **Example:** *"In my previous board role, we placed a strong emphasis on maintaining **director independence** to ensure that our decisions were made objectively and in the best interests of the company. I was particularly conscious of this when we were evaluating major strategic initiatives that might benefit certain stakeholders. We took the time to identify potential conflicts of interest, and I recused myself from discussions where I had a personal or professional connection that could cloud my judgment."*

Director Liability—Legal obligations and potential consequences for actions taken as a board member.

> **Example:** *"We ensured that all board members were well-educated on their responsibilities, particularly around corporate governance and compliance, to minimize risks and protect both the company and individual board members from **director liability**."*

Directors and Officers (D&O) Insurance—Provides financial protection for board members against legal claims. Both corporate firms and nonprofit organizations (those with a fiduciary duty) should provide D&O insurance for their board members.

> **Example:** *"As a board member, I worked closely with our legal and risk management teams to ensure that our **D&O insurance policy** provided the appropriate level of coverage for all board members. My legal expertise in the insurance industry was called upon to review the policy details to ensure they covered key risks associated with our industry, including litigation risks and potential regulatory investigations."*

Chapter 4 ▪ Preparing Your Brand

Equity Compensation—The practice of offering board members ownership in the company, typically in the form of stock options or shares, which aligns their interests with the company's long-term performance and shareholder value.

> **Example:** *"In my role on the compensation committee, I was involved in revamping our **equity compensation** guidelines to better align the interests of the board with the long-term goals of the company. We reviewed the existing structure, which primarily offered stock options, and decided to introduce performance-based stock grants to further motivate senior executives. The new approach not only drove shareholder value but ensured that compensation was directly tied to the company's sustained growth and success."*

Executive Sessions—Private meetings of the board without company management (including the CEO) present, often used to discuss sensitive matters that require confidentiality. Mellody Hobson, board member and Co-CEO of Ariel Investments, shared at the Economic Club of Chicago in December 2024 that one of her public company boards holds an executive session after every board meeting. This private time allows the board to reflect on the discussions and outcomes of the meeting in order to seek alignment and address any sensitive matters. Topics often covered in these sessions include reviewing quarterly or annual reports, evaluating leadership performance and compensation, refining leadership development strategies, planning for CEO succession, conducting board self-assessments, discussing security threats and crisis-response plans, and addressing legal matters.

> **Example:** *"During my tenure on a nonprofit board, we held **executive sessions** to focus on how we could better support the executive director's development. We would also discuss public relations crises that came up. With my media and legal background, I was able to provide deeper insights during these discussions, contributing to the organization's brand awareness and resilience."*

Independent Director—A board member who doesn't have a significant relationship with the company and can make impartial decisions. (This designation is often defined by the SEC or the company itself.)

> **Example:** *"As an **independent director** on the board of a tech start-up, I was able to provide objective input on key decisions such as new product development and strategic partnerships without any conflicts of interest. Since I had no direct financial or personal ties to the company, I could offer a fresh perspective without any external pressures or biases to help ensure that decisions were made in the best interest of all stakeholders. This impartiality was critical in maintaining the board's integrity and upholding the company's commitment to transparency and governance standards."*

Nomination Process—The procedure for evaluating and appointing the CEO (and, at times, the CFO and other C-suite roles) and new board members.

> **Example:** *"During my time on the nominating/governance committee, we conducted a thorough **nomination process** to select new board members. I liaised directly with a search consultant to define the role and seek out an initial list of candidates. We evaluated candidates based on their expertise, leadership experience, and alignment with our company's values, and after reviewing resumes/board bios and conducting interviews, we presented the final candidates to the full board for a vote. This structured process ensured that the new director would bring meaningful value and complement the skills of existing members."*

Onboarding—The process in which directors are welcomed onto the board and introduced to the business and other directors and officers.

> **Example:** *"I was in charge of completely revamping the **onboarding process** for new board members. I developed a 'board book' which included the last five years of financials, minutes from the last eight board meetings, an organizational chart, and other essential reports that helped new board members assimilate more quickly."*

Overboarded—Someone who is on too many boards and can't keep up with their director duties.

> **Example:** *"I once served alongside a director who was **overboarded**. She was sitting on eight different boards at the same time. Despite her vast experience, it became clear that she was struggling to devote the necessary time and energy to each role. She had difficulty attending meetings regularly, and her input started to feel less impactful. The company eventually addressed this issue by discussing the need for her to step back from some of her other commitments to focus more on our board."*

Crafting your accomplishments using relevant board language will demonstrate how your successes align with the responsibilities of a board director. In addition, the more you comprehend the legal and ethical responsibilities of board membership, including duty of care, duty of loyalty, duty of obedience, and the overall governance framework, the easier it will be to demonstrate your board readiness.

4. Enhance Your Online Presence

Once you are clear on the value you would bring as a board director and how your accomplishments are relevant to serving on a board, you will want to make sure that your online presence matches your brand.

- **Social media cleanse:** Be intentional in all of your social media interactions on sites such as LinkedIn, Instagram, Facebook, TikTok, X, Threads, and BlueSky. Demonstrate a senior level *presence* and relevant experiences. This may require you to "scrub" your platforms of anything that could be considered controversial, too opinionated, or inappropriate (e.g., party photos, politically polarizing posts). Make sure all of your profile pictures look similar so there is brand consistency.

- **Content posting:** Social media, especially LinkedIn, is an underutilized but powerful tool in your board search strategy. While networking and personal introductions are still critical, your content serves as a digital extension of your brand, reflecting not only what you know but how you think.

When you are seeking a board seat, your goal is to shift your public narrative from "operator" to "strategic advisor." This means you are no longer "doing" the work. You are advising on the overall business. Posting regularly on governance-related topics using board-level language also signals to your network (and to potential nomination committees) that you are already thinking like a director.

As you make these revisions, focus on sharing board-relevant insights grounded in your own experience. For example:

- Strategic planning and transformation initiatives
- Risk management and oversight responsibilities
- Lessons from organizational leadership
- Industry trends, disruptions, and how boards should respond
- Challenges facing CEOs or boards and how directors can add value

The goal is to change your language to something that qualifies you to comment on boardroom decisions: "Check out this new legislation on [issue]. It will be interesting to see how it will impact how boards think about . . ."

Keeping a consistent posting rhythm shows engagement and creates momentum. We recommend posting once or twice a week with a focus on governance, leadership, and oversight. Think about your content as *positioning*, not just commentary. Pair this with short reflections, articles, or original thought pieces that convey your point of view. Importantly, this is not about self-promotion; it's about demonstrating thought leadership. Here are some examples of how you can expand your social reach and position yourself as a potential board member:

- **Teach something:** "Here's a 3-step way to approach risk management . . ."

- **Share insight:** "This stat caught my eye. Here's why it will matter in boardrooms."
- **Reaction posts:** "I read this article on [topic]. Here's where I agree/disagree."
- **Board interaction:** "Every time I present to a board, I consider these three things to ensure that my presentation is thoughtful, actionable, and creates conversation."
- **Humble brag wins:** "I led a cross-functional initiative that reduced operational risk by 30%. It was a great reminder that sustainable growth starts with discipline and staying aligned with strategic goals."

Remember to stay on brand of "being a board candidate." Avoid diluting your message by switching gears to topics like job-hunting tips for junior analysts or celebrating a team lunch. Keep your lens elevated and strategic and make sure you are using boardroom language in your posts such as "fiduciary responsibility," "enterprise risk," "stakeholder value," "capital allocation," and "long-term strategy."

We get asked all the time, "Do I have to post? Does it actually help?" Our answer is always a resounding, "Yes!" Here's what thoughtful posting can do:

- Increases visibility and engagement on your profile
- Keeps you top-of-mind when a board opportunity arises
- Reengages dormant contacts or influencers in your network
- Shows you are actively tracking the issues boards are concerned with

Think of LinkedIn as an updated mobile phone contact list or Rolodex (for those who remember those!) with the ability to communicate with your audience in real time.

If you are not a social media aficionado, ask an AI program such as ChatGPT for post ideas using prompts such as, "I am seeking a board position and I am an expert in business transformation. Give me ideas for thought leadership posts regarding business transformation using board-ready language versus executive language."

Most importantly, don't just copy/paste responses from AI programs. They sound stiff, are written in a certain pattern, and may not sound like you! Writing in your unique voice is the key to creating connection, generating authentic insights, and establishing your brand. In addition to posting, take note of your comments on other people's posts, and the posts that you engage with. Your activity is visible to everyone.

→ **Other platforms/channels:** You could consider creating a blog, or a LinkedIn newsletter to showcase your expertise and insights on board-related topics. You may also want to participate in webinars or podcasts to share your knowledge and connect with other leaders in your field.

Find the modality that feels authentic to you. Remember, the objective is to engage publicly in a way that demonstrates your knowledge and expertise to establish credibility. It's not to become a social media or SEO expert.

5. Own Your Brand

Once you've established your brand, you are prepared to own your readiness to be on a board. It is now time to surround yourself with like-minded people who will support you.

→ **Masterminds:** These are like-minded people who help each other achieve their goals. Consider joining board "masterminds" such as CEO roundtable groups or groups that speak to the C-suite like HerCsuite, Tiger21, or Vistage. These are helpful environments for gaining additional knowledge about how to position yourself and establishing new contacts who can make introductions at this level.

→ **Board education groups:** Organizations that discuss the latest governance networks and training are great places to connect with like-minded individuals and gain insights. One resource that we recommend in particular is called Directors & Boards.[1] Furthermore, stay up to date on best practices in corporate governance by attending workshops, speaking events, and webinars. During board interviews, you will be grateful for having learned from experts in governance when you are able to provide your opinion on current board-level topics.

→ **Mentorship:** Seek out mentors who are experienced board directors to gain advice and guidance on navigating your board journey. Pay close attention to Chapter 7 to know when and when not to ask your network for advice. It's important to approach your network only when you are board-ready.

Following the above steps will ensure that you have created a strong personal brand and presence that speaks to board directors in their language, shows board readiness, and positions you as a compelling candidate for board director roles.

Chapter 4 Summary

1. **Identify core accomplishments:** Write down your accomplishments through the lens of growth, transformation, and risk.

2. **Articulate your unique value proposition:** To truly stand out on a board, focus on the distinctive expertise or experience that only you can bring to the table.

3. **Master board language:** Enhance your accomplishments with board language and keywords to position yourself as a credible potential board member.

4. **Enhance your online presence:** Build and fine-tune your online presence by writing posts, articles, and/or newsletters about subjects relevant to board service and commenting on

other board-relevant posts to establish board-level thought leadership.

5. **Own your brand:** Surround yourself with like-minded people who are either board members or think like board members and who can provide you the influential network you need for the future.

CHAPTER

Board Materials

"A board seat is not merely achieved. It is secured through precise strategic positioning. Your bio, résumé, and digital presence must act as a high-level ambassador, projecting credibility, influence, and foresight before you ever enter the room."

—Wendy O. Brown, board member and retired lieutenant colonel, NATO

Once you've clarified your motivations and values, learned all you can about the nature of board service, and built your brand as a strong board director candidate, it's time to craft the right materials and hone your pitch to showcase your qualifications, experience, and unique value. Your board bio, board-focused resume, executive resume, LinkedIn profile, and even your professional image must all align to tell a cohesive story of why you are board-ready.

In this chapter, we'll guide you in creating materials that reflect your governance mindset, emphasize your leadership strengths, and ensure that you stand out in a competitive field. With the right preparation, you'll be equipped to make a confident and lasting impression.

Tip #5: Board materials need to say at first glance that you are board-ready.

Most Requested Board Documents

One of the most common questions we receive is, "What documents do I need when interviewing for a board position?" Some boards like more formal documents that they can deeply dig into, while others want a document that is short and to the point and that answers the question, "What will you do for me?" Over the years, we have found that each industry and company want something a little different. They may tell you in advance (which is most helpful) and they may not.

Your board documents will demonstrate to an influential contact that you are board-ready, or they may be used to apply for a board position in a more formal setting. You will also need a "leave behind"—a concise board profile of your skills, experience, and value you bring—for people that you meet or reconnect with, but for formal applications, a different set of documents may be required.

The list on the next page is not definitive because some search consultants and companies require a specific format, but it's broad enough to give you a good idea of what different types of boards might expect from candidates.

Board *search consultants* also need a board bio and an executive resume (two pages maximum) with current board director experience listed at the top. Some search consultants will create a profile for you so that all candidates are uniformly presented to their client.

The Board Bio

A board biography (bio) is a person's history and experience in narrative format, highlighting a candidate's skills and experience to demonstrate their suitability for a board position. It is not a repurposed executive bio or resume because it is not a chronology of everything you have done *as an executive*. It *is* one of the toughest documents to write. Not many professional resume writers are able to produce a great board bio, so consult with experts on this particular document.

Your board bio is a clear articulation of your personal value proposition (the unique contributions you will bring to a board), substantiated

Board Document Requirements	Public Co Large Cap	Public Co Mid Cap	Public Co Small Cap	Private: PE Backed	Private: ESOP	Private: Family-Owned	Private: Founder-Owned	Mutual Fund	Start-up	Nonprofit	Advisory Board
Board Bio	X	X	X		X	X	X	X		X	
Board Resume (1 page)				X		X	X	X	X	X	X
Executive Resume (with board experience included)	X	X	X	X	X	X	X	X	X	X	X
Values Summary					X	X					
Governance Experience	X	X	X		X	X		X		X	

X = general requirement for applying for board seats

with your career experiences, accomplishments, and skills. Similar to developing an elevator pitch (which you will read about in Chapter 6), you should create a bio in the third person (as if you are talking about someone else—in this case yourself!) that provides general background, describes your value proposition, explains your board experience, and ends with a bit of personal information. For example, think about starting paragraphs with phrases like, "Randy is qualified to lead a board discussion on . . ." or "As a board director, Ellen brings . . ." The final paragraph of a board bio should include some personal information written a bit like this: "Brian enjoys spending time with his family in Chicago, following a healthy lifestyle, and working outdoors. His interests include reading, automobiles, and investment trends."

There is no need to go into detail about career highlights from years ago. Here's an example of a bio where the board candidate's first position is summarized in two board-ready sentences: "Katherine launched her career at IBM and ascended through more than twelve promotions into roles of increasing scope. Her work there emphasized corporate strategy and finance, enterprise transformations, operational optimization, and capital markets and investments."

This is what to include in a board bio:

→ A board-ready headshot (see details on headshots below)

→ Your phone number, email, and LinkedIn URL

→ Your city and state (US) or your city and country if it's relevant to the boards you are seeking to join (more common in Europe or internationally)

→ A summary list of your subject matter expertise

The example on page 85 puts it all together.

The Board Resume

As mentioned earlier in this chapter, not all boards require a board bio. Some board search consultants and boards prefer a board resume (aka "board CV"), which is a one- or two-page document with more details about your experience but through the lens of a board director. This means identifying your most relevant achievements and roles and describing them as they relate to board-level topics.

Some people think they can leverage their current resume to help create their board resume, but for boards, it's not as simple as that. Since your executive resume describes what you have accomplished as an executive, and the role of a board member requires a different skill set, the goal is to develop your board resume in a different template with new language.

For example, your current resume may read, "Led a cross-functional team of 200+ employees to implement a $50M digital transformation project, resulting in a 30% increase in operational efficiency and annual

Jacqueline T. Shawhacker

Location, State • 555-555-5555 • email • LinkedIn Profile

Board-Ready Strategist Driving Financial Resilience, Governance Excellence, and Growth in ESOP Enterprises

Jacqueline T. Shawhacker is an executive and governance leader with expertise in employee stock ownership plans (ESOPs), corporate finance, and strategic growth. With over 25 years of experience driving value creation in employee-owned businesses, Jacqueline brings financial acumen, operational leadership, and governance insight to the boardroom.

Currently, Jacqueline serves as an independent advisor to ESOP-owned companies, helping them navigate executive succession planning, capital structuring, and governance best practices to ensure long-term sustainability and employee engagement. Previously, she was the chief financial officer at [company name], a 100% employee-owned manufacturing firm, where she led the transition to ESOP ownership, securing long-term financial stability and enhancing employee participation in corporate decision-making.

Financial Expertise

Risk and Crisis Management

Growth Strategy

Business Transformation

Regulatory Compliance

Prior, Jacqueline was the senior vice president of corporate strategy at [company name], where she advised mid-market firms on ESOP feasibility, M&A transactions, and shareholder transitions. She also held leadership roles at [company name], focusing on investment strategies for employee-owned businesses, and at [company name], where she spearheaded financial planning initiatives that optimized shareholder value. Jacqueline is qualified to chair an audit and risk committee and would be an active member of a compensation committee.

In board governance, Jacqueline has chaired the boards of the National Center for Employee Ownership (NCEO) and the ESOP Association. She has also served on various advisory boards for multiple employee-owned organizations, mentoring CEOs on how to achieve profitable growth.

Jacqueline holds an MBA from the Wharton School of the University of Pennsylvania and is a frequent speaker on governance, finance, and strategic planning for ESOPs. Her ability to bridge the gap between executive leadership and board oversight makes her a valuable asset to any ESOP board looking to enhance financial resilience, operational excellence, and employee engagement.

Jacqueline enjoys spending time with her family, which includes her husband and three teenage children, and competing in triathlons, marathons, and other long-distance races.

cost savings of $10 million." When communicating those achievements through the lens of a board role, it might look like this: "Advised the executive team on strategic oversight and governance of a $50-million digital transformation project, ensuring alignment with long-term business objectives and risk management practices." The executive version emphasizes hands-on leadership, direct management, and execution of a major project; the board version focuses on strategic oversight, advisory roles, and governance, highlighting how you would guide, review, and ensure compliance and alignment with broader company goals. This shift in emphasis demonstrates the applicant's readiness to contribute to a board by framing their expertise in terms of insight, guidance, and high-level stewardship rather than operational detail.

Even if a particular accomplishment doesn't seem impressive within the scope of your executive role, consider how it translates to a higher-level oversight perspective. For example, when Marlo led the production risk team at a major cable company, her role involved managing reality show risk. While this responsibility may not appear to be directly relevant to a board position, reframing it to highlight the strategic essence reveals its value: "Proven track record of exceptional judgment and strategic oversight to mitigate organizational risk through innovative solutions to complex, high-stakes crises, resulting in multimillion-dollar cost savings." This phrasing captures the core impact of that work, demonstrating her ability to contribute to a board with high-level strategic insight and risk management expertise without delving into granular day-to-day details.

In building your board resume/CV, include the following in this order:

- → Short summary (to grab the reader)
- → Board specialties (your subject matter expertise)
- → Board experience
- → Executive experience or competencies that summarize the accomplishments related to board roles
- → Education
- → Awards (only the ones that are relevant)

Do not include the following:

→ A book you wrote that wasn't about governance or anything related to boards

→ An award you achieved for something more than 20 years ago

→ Speaking engagements (especially where the topic is not board related)

→ Television appearances (especially where the topic is not board related)

→ Certifications that aren't used at the board level (e.g., project management)

→ Too many governance certifications (These can make you look like you understand theory but have no real-world practice; list only the most relevant ones.)

An example of a board director candidate resume is shown on pages 88 and 89.

Leveraging LinkedIn

Your LinkedIn profile *must* attract board search consultants, and it all starts with your photo. Your photo will either broadcast "board director" or something else, such as executive, public speaker, or . . . nothing. The following suggestions will ensure that your headshot projects the right board director image and nothing less:

1. Choose appropriate board attire. Choose clothing that reflects boardroom professionalism, typically a well-tailored suit in neutral or attire in bold colors that signal authority. Men may opt for a sports jacket over a shirt and no tie or a more formal dress code. Women will want to pay close attention to the collar on their suit or blazer. Don't pick a blazer with a traditional collar; find a collarless option known as a "lapel-less blazer" from Anne Taylor, Chico's, or a major department store like Lord & Taylor. These usually come in two primary neck styles—a deep V-neck or a round neck with buttons—and give more of a board-vibe than an executive vibe.

NAME

Los Angeles, CA • email • 555-555-5555 • email • LinkedIn

BOARD DIRECTOR | FINANCIAL EXPERT

Chief financial officer with a career of leading best-in-class financial management spanning multiple industries in both public and private companies. Strategic advisor on all matters related to SOX, ERM, and corporate governance for public companies and their audit committees as well as private, pre-IPO firms. Adept at evaluating and enhancing internal controls, driving continuous improvement, and ensuring regulatory compliance across current and emerging risks. Committed to communication and collaboration to meet an organization's ethos, vision, and mission. Financial expert and Agile leader qualified to serve on audit, risk, compensation, nom/gov, and investment committees.

BOARD EXPERTISE

Financial Expert • Retail & Distribution • Risk Mitigation • Corporate Governance • Human Capital • Shareholder Relations • CEO Compensation • Operational Management • Change Management • ESG • Cybersecurity

BOARD-LEVEL EXPERIENCE

CFO/Executive Board Director, Attend Audit Committee Meetings   2022–Current
Company Name A, (NYSE: COMA)

Board Member, Member, Audit Committee   2013–2022
Company Name B

Board Member and Co-Chair of Fundraising Committee   2013–2019
Nonprofit Name

COMPETENCY FOCUS

Growth

- **Financial resilience:** Oversight of significant enhancements and efficiencies in cash flow management, optimizing sales processes, and working capital utilization across both public and private sectors, resulting in strengthened financial resilience and sustainable growth.
- **Growth optimization:** Spearheaded operational effectiveness strategies driving expansion, growth, and efficiencies, resulting in optimized resource utilization and increased profitability.
- **IPO readiness:** Prepared [company name] for an initial public offering, overseeing financial, operational, market, investor, and governance readiness.
- **Business transformation:** Drove M&A initiatives with a focus on transformation and integration, emphasizing human capital optimization.

Name page 2 of 2

Strategic Risk Management

- **Governance:** Advanced effective corporate governance by aligning practices with board standards, fostering transparency and accountability, and ensuring ethical oversight while actively shaping audit committee agendas and monitoring compliance with the audit charter to uphold regulatory integrity.
- **Digital transformation:** Directed digital transformation and enterprise change initiatives, including reverse logistics optimization and modernization of operational accounting systems, resulting in reduced inventory waste and improved regulatory compliance across the organization.
- **Enterprise risk management:** Led the design and implementation of a comprehensive enterprise risk management (ERM) framework, embedding risk intelligence into decision-making, and oversaw the creation of a cybersecurity incident response plan to fortify organizational resilience and board-level risk oversight.

CAREER CHRONOLOGY

Chief Financial Officer, *Company A, Los Angeles, CA*	2022–Current
VP, Finance, *Company B, Columbus, OH*	2013–2022
Senior Auditor, *Company C, Naperville, IL*	2012–2013
Internal Audit Manager (Chief Audit Executive), *Company D, Itasca, IL*	2006–2012
Associate, *Company E, New York City, NY*	2004–2006
Intern Accountant, *Company F, Raleigh, NC*	2002–2004

EDUCATION & QUALIFICATIONS

Master of Business Administration (MBA), Cum Laude
University of Miami, Coral Gables, FL

Bachelor of Science, Accounting & Finance, Magna Cum Laude
Yale University, New Haven, CT

Certified Public Accountant (CPA)

Always consider the type of board you are looking to join. If you are joining a tech start-up advisory board, for example, a suit and tie might not be appropriate. Take various clothing options with you to the photo shoot and remember to focus on what your audience wants!

2. Choose a neutral/plain background. The background should be a plain wall or a photographer's professional backdrop that contrasts with what you are wearing (e.g., light if you are wearing a dark top or dark if you are wearing a more neutral color).

3. Focus on lighting and clarity. Good lighting that enhances your features without harsh shadows is essential. Make sure that the image is sharp and high-resolution, conveying attention to detail.

4. Use a professional photographer. Hire a professional for the best results. They'll guide you on posing, lighting, and framing that align with your goals. But don't just choose any "headshot" photographer; find one who has taken pictures of board members or of people who have successfully achieved a board position. They understand the type of look you are trying to convey.

Here are some ways to determine if a photographer has the right skills to take a great board headshot:

- Look on their website for a section called "Headshots." Some photographers focus on weddings or families; they are not typically board photographers. The ones who do headshots will have a section for this specific type of picture.
- Their headshots should look professional, not like the fun shots couples do for their engagement.
- Their headshots should capture the unique personality of the person in the photo. This is key.

Consider looking at board member photos on company websites of your favorite brands and note their clothing, facial expressions, lighting, and how they compare to their *executive* professional headshots such as those on their company website if they are still working in a professional capacity.

5. **Project confidence and approachability.** You may notice in your board photo research that each person has a friendly but modest smile, the corners of their mouth angled upwards. When looking at the camera, lean in a bit and slightly upturn the corners of your lips so you are almost smiling. It's like saying, "I got you." Project authority in your picture so people know you are ready to be on a board. This will be a very different photo than any you have taken before.

From our experience, we haven't found AI pictures to be very reliable, so don't focus on saving money on your clothes or a photographer. This is one of the most senior level roles in an organization, so spending the money is worth it!

LinkedIn Background Banner

The background banner to the photo should be simple and plain. You can even match it with some of the colors in your photo background or your clothing so the image looks aligned and branded. Here are a few examples (while these are in black, white, and grey, you can make them in any color that feels right to you and exemplifies executive such as dark blues and greens):

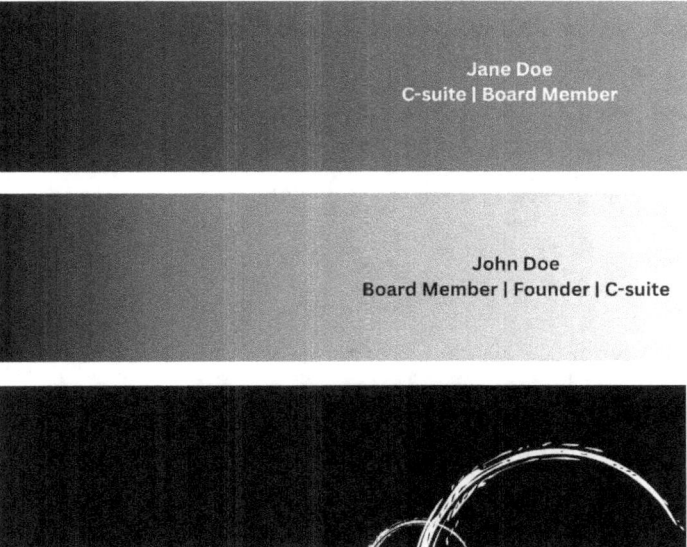

Some people choose to add a personal photo of a sunset or a skyline of the city they live in or have visited. Be careful that these pictures don't give the wrong impression such as that of a Bourbon Street partier or a Zen-like retirement. Refrain from writing quotes or inspirational messages—you never know how these will be interpreted.

Your name. Use your formal name on your LinkedIn profile, e.g., no initials or informalities such as "J. P." or "Christy" when your name is Christina. Further, don't add "ex-Google," "ex-Meta," or any certification, license, or academic credentials after your name such as PhD, JD, MBA, etc. These are fine for an executive, but you are seeking a board director position, so your name should be enough. Trust us: Search consultants and board members will review your entire profile multiple times before they meet you.

Your headline. Your headline should have keywords in it such as "strategic" or "governance" or "risk." A simple one to use is "Strategic Advisor" (although, technically, all executives are strategic advisors). If you are already in the C-suite, then add your chief title, such as "CFO" or "CMO." If you are not in the C-suite, consider your experience in the context of a board role such as "Risk Management Executive," "Governance Expert," or "Strategic Leader." Keep your list between three and six items. Any more will confuse the reader. You are trying to create a brand!

Example:
NAME
Strategic Advisor | CFO/Financial Expert | Risk Management | Governance | Regulatory | Compliance Expert

About section. Be sure to add an About section in your LinkedIn profile. In studying more than 100 LinkedIn profiles from experienced board directors, one of the common themes is that the About section is short:

two-to-three concise paragraphs only, which includes relevant information not only about you and your experiences, but about previous companies you worked for that align with your board member aspirations. (You can also bullet-point key highlights that are relevant to board oversight.) For example:

> I was named chief financial officer of [company name] in 2021 and later took on the role of chair of the board at [company name] in 2022, serving in that capacity until today. I also serve on the audit, nomination, and technology committees.
>
> During my tenure as CFO at [company name], the business grew to more than $25 billion in revenue and became a global leader in enterprise software solutions, serving over 100,000 businesses worldwide. [Company name], formerly known as [previous company name] and now operating as [current company name], specializes in cloud computing, cybersecurity, and AI-driven analytics.
>
> In board governance, I serve on the board of directors of [start-up company name] and [nonprofit company name]. Passionate about local business and mentorship, I co-founded and serve on the board of the [state] Hispanic Chamber of Commerce.

Right after the final paragraph in About, add a section called Specialties that lists relevant career keywords and subject matter expertise.

> **Specialties**
> C-suite | Financial Expert | Software Technology | CPA | Governance Cybersecurity Risk | Start-ups

Education. Complete the Education section with all formal degrees, including undergraduate and graduate degrees. Put graduate degrees at the top, followed by your undergraduate degree, then any short courses at the bottom. When you first open a LinkedIn profile, you only see the top two entries for education. Therefore, it's important that certificates or courses from universities aren't featured, because if board members and board search consultants see short courses first, it won't create the impact you are looking for. First impressions endure! Even if you took advanced education courses or gained certifications at Ivy League schools but only attended a midrange school for your undergraduate degree, courses and certifications still go at the bottom. Don't worry! Not all board members went to Ivy League schools.

Licenses and certifications. These are absolutely relevant to board consideration. If you are a licensed lawyer, you know governance and risk. If you are certified in HR, you may have expertise in human capital strategies. If you have a Financial Industry Regulatory Authority (FINRA) license, you will be seen as having finance, governance, and risk management experience. Even a coaching certification shows you know how to communicate in a way that is constructive and strategic. One piece of advice: Review this list on a regular basis. If you received the most basic certification 15 years ago but now have a more advanced license, you may want to remove the original certification as long as it is understood that it was a requirement for taking the next step. If a list of certifications is too long, you run the risk of creating confusion for the reader.

Skills. Remember that the skills and capabilities needed for your executive roles (operational) are completely different from those needed when seeking a board position (governance). Therefore, "rebrand" those skills to reflect your experience in risk management, financial oversight, governance, and strategic transformation.

This provides another opportunity to note any areas of expertise that might be missing from your executive experience and consider building those skills over the coming months.

Recommendations. These are essential to helping a board search committee understand more about you. You will want recommendations that reflect how you provide strategic guidance, understand certain industries and markets, provide transformation oversight, handled financial risk and risk management, and so on. Remove old recommendations and seek out new ones from people at the board or C level. If you are on a nonprofit board, ask one of the other board members (preferably the chair) to provide a written reference that speaks to your role on the board.

When requesting LinkedIn recommendations that reflect your board capabilities, you might ask your recommenders to focus on certain key areas. For example:

> I would greatly appreciate it if you could speak to my ability to provide strategic oversight, especially in times of transformation. Highlighting how I've contributed to shaping high-level decisions that drive business growth, innovation, and operational efficiency would be especially valuable. Additionally, I'd really appreciate it if you included my experience in governance and how I ensured that organizational processes aligned with best practices and regulatory standards. Please also mention my expertise in risk mitigation and management, particularly in navigating complex situations and protecting the company's interests while enabling progress. Your insights into how I've guided the organization through these areas while keeping a focus on the long-term vision would be incredibly impactful.

This request will help your recommenders focus on the strategic and governance aspects that align with board-level responsibilities.

Instead of asking someone to write a recommendation from scratch, and to make sure you receive a strong recommendation, offer to provide a draft, and then tell them to feel free to edit it. This will save them a lot of time and give the recommender a better understanding of exactly what you are looking for.

Chapter 5 Summary

1. **Board bio:** Create a narrative document that highlights your skills and experience through the lens of growth, transformation, and risk to demonstrate your suitability for a board position.

2. **Board resume:** Create a resume that highlights your board expertise, board-level experience (including presenting to boards), career chronology, competency, education, qualifications, licenses, and certifications.

3. **Leveraging LinkedIn:** Create a dynamic profile that demonstrates your expertise, skills, and experience but also projects an image of you as a legitimate board member via your headshot picture, background, and About section.

CHAPTER

Board Pitch Prep

"Getting on a board isn't only about credentials. It's about demonstrating board-level thinking. Engage in governance discussions, contribute your expertise, and take on advisory roles to build credibility. Board opportunities will follow when you're seen as a strategic leader."

—Cathy Skala, board member and former international healthcare executive

You are now ready to demonstrate the value you can bring to a board, but what exactly does that mean? To convince someone that you would be successful serving on their board, you will need to build a strong and confident pitch that will impress them enough to take you seriously—even when you have little-to-no experience. In other words, you need to *tell* them what your value is and why that value is needed.

Tip #6: Own your value, lead with purpose, and project board-ready confidence.

Your pitch has to be clear, concise, and to the point because you will only have about 30-to-90 seconds to get your value proposition across to someone.

Here are the three ways to make sure that you present yourself as board-ready:

Presenting Yourself as Board Ready

1. Exude Confidence.

Being confident in the value you would bring to a board is one of the most important ways to impress the people you speak to. Without that confidence, a person of influence is unlikely to refer you to a board or back your candidacy. Confidence is also demonstrated by having a clear understanding of which boards are best suited for you and conveying your value proposition both verbally and with a strong executive presence—no stumbling or hesitation! Bringing confidence to every meeting, call, conversation, and interview will increase your chances of being referred, selected, or engaged with the right people on your way to securing a board position.

Not long ago, Naomi worked with an executive who had spent an entire year trying to get on a board. Despite having many conversations with his network, he was getting frustrated with the process and was ready to give up. He had a great career history, worked at multiple Fortune 100 companies, and held a C-suite title for many years. "Why am I getting nowhere?" he wondered. When Naomi asked what he'd been saying on these calls and in these meetings, he said, "I've been asking my network if they think I would be a good board candidate and what they think I should do, trying to get their expert advice." This executive wasn't in the exploratory phase; he was stuck in the "trying to get on a board" phase. He was doing what a lot of people do—asking their network for validation and/or direction—but this approach doesn't create a sense of confidence. It made his listeners think he was unsure of his direction and unclear about what he would bring to a board. As a result, he was getting no referrals or references for board positions. After changing his approach and creating a confident narrative, he secured a board seat in just six months. He stopped asking his network for advice and started telling them the direction he was going and what he was going to achieve.

2. Translate Expertise into Board-Relevant Value.

You've built a compelling narrative of your accomplishments using board language; now it's time to ensure those achievements align with what boards actually need.

Let's revisit the golf analogy. Imagine you show up for a round of golf with a group but all you talk about is how great you are at tennis. Sure, there are similarities. Both involve a ball, require skill, are played outside (mainly), and use an instrument to hit the ball. But while your tennis expertise is impressive, it doesn't tell the golfers anything about how well you would play *their* game.

The same applies to board readiness. Your achievements may be exceptional as an operator, but if they don't clearly translate to governance, fiduciary responsibility, risk oversight, or strategic decision-making, your audience may not see how they apply to the boardroom. Ensuring your expertise is framed through a board-relevant lens is key to demonstrating your value as a board member.

To position yourself effectively, avoid highlighting aspects of your career that don't resonate with board responsibilities. For example:

→ **People management or CRM implementation:** While valuable in an executive role, these are not board-level concerns.

→ **Consulting jargon:** Terms like "projects," "delivering reports," or "client solutions" are not board-relevant and can dilute your positioning.

Instead, reframe your experience. Boards don't execute; they advise, govern, and oversee. Shift your language accordingly:

→ Use "**oversee**" instead of "**manage**."

→ Use "**advise**" instead of "**execute**."

→ Use "**provide strategic guidance**" instead of "**deliver reports**."

By aligning your expertise with the priorities of a board, you will demonstrate that your value is both clear and compelling.

3. Know Your Audience.

We talked earlier about taking time to research the boards you want to join and understanding the roles and responsibilities of board members. Now, take this a step further and more deeply engage the people you are speaking to by making your pitch relevant to them. Knowing your audience and what they care about is an essential part of the process.

A full-time professor from the University of Chicago we'll call Joe decided he wanted to join a corporate board. He knew how important it was to know his audience, so during interviews, he used his subject matter expertise and unique value proposition to his advantage. The company was in the research and development stage of a brand-new technology in the solar power industry. They were looking for advisory board members to guide them through their first two years. Joe spoke to the founder/CEO, and after learning what the company needed, he described how bringing him onto the board would help the company find the best way to design their research capabilities and launch their product. He also had experience with grants, fundraising, and working with local officials to whom he could make introductions. Finally, he offered his school's research lab and state-of-the-art equipment if the company needed it. This all resonated with the founder/CEO, and after a few more meetings to discuss the research and the professor's ideas, he was offered a position on the board.

Pitch Format

Once you grasp the underlying strategy behind the pitch, create one with your best value proposition. There are no rules for pitches, but here's a simple format to get you started:

1. What Is Your Overall Board Brand?

When interviewing for a job, you typically present your experience in reverse chronological order, starting with your earliest roles and building toward your current expertise. In a board interview, however, you do the opposite. You lead with who you are today, emphasizing the value you would bring to a boardroom setting.

When answering an open-ended question like, "Can you tell me a little about yourself?" your response should be concise, compelling, and framed in board language. This is your opportunity to engage the interviewer and position yourself as a strategic asset. For example:

> I am currently the chief financial officer of [company name], a publicly traded company with a [$ cap] in the [industry] sector. I am also a board member. I bring expertise in financial oversight, risk management, and compliance with a strong background in M&A and private equity. My career began in investment banking at Morgan Stanley, Goldman Sachs, and other firms followed by leadership roles in hedge funds and corporate finance. This experience allowed me to provide strategic financial insights, ensure strong governance, and support long-term value creation. In addition, I have worked closely with audit committees and advised on capital allocation, making me well-versed in the fiduciary responsibilities critical to board service.

This structure highlights your board-relevant expertise while keeping the response direct and engaging.

2. What Are the Three Things You Bring to This Specific Board?

Think about what CEOs and boards care about most: growth and stability, mitigating risk, and transformation, such as the ability to pivot a company in response to changing conditions. Prepare a statement on each of these areas so you can speak to each one.

Further, from your research, try to predict what may be impacting a particular company. Is it market competition? Government regulatory clearances? How AI will impact their business? Find three areas where your direct experience and expertise will bring exceptional value to the board. Here are a few examples:

> With increasing competition in your market, my experience in identifying new revenue streams can help bring unique value to your organization and strengthen your market position to ensure sustainable, long-term growth.

Given the regulatory challenges in your industry, my experience working with government agencies and specifically the FDA in navigating complex compliance landscapes can help ensure the board is equipped to strategically address these hurdles.

3. Describe Your Board Experience.
(Don't skip this section even if you have no board experience!)

Yes, this may be something you have never done before or needed to, but since you are seeking a board role, it's important to highlight any board experience as this is most relatable to board search consultants and nominating committee members.

When describing your board history, focus on which experiences stand out: the M&A, the CEO succession, the expansion, the committees you served on, and any investor situations such as activist initiatives. Boards like to see that you have been through tough times and know how to handle a crisis. Board members need to be resilient!

And what if you have NO board experience? That's okay! Being transparent with boards is very important, but here some of the things you can describe instead and how to say it:

I don't have *direct* board experience, however:

- I have presented to a board.
- I have attended a board meeting (or a board committee meeting).
- I have extensive knowledge of corporate governance.
- I have been on a committee where I had to collaborate with others to complete a project.

If none of the options above work for you, consider taking some extra time (e.g., the next 3–6 months or even longer) to build board-relevant experience in your corporate career before launching your board career. It can be as simple as joining a meeting or getting involved in a strategic initiative.

In Chapter 1, we discussed the importance of aligning your values to the boards you want to join. Disclosing your values at the board level may only be required when you are interviewing or having lengthier discussions about your board career with high-level influencers. However, doing so is a clear indication that you are aware of your responsibilities and are board-ready. Also, don't recite the values you think you have (or worse, "I am known for . . ."") but start instead with something more direct and positive: "As a board member, I value the duty of care and loyalty, and I value boards that desire innovative market insights."

If you are applying for a *nonprofit* board role, communicate your values during all interactions with the board or other volunteers. For example, "I value education, and believe that all children throughout our community should have access to the best after-school programs." If you are seeking a nonprofit board position for the first time, we recommend describing your ability to fundraise and even the extensiveness of your support network.

4. Tell Your Audience About the Type of Board Culture That Fits Best with Your Experience.

Tell as many people as possible about your desire to join a corporate or nonprofit board. Use your board-ready elevator pitch to remind them about the kind of board member you are or want to be, and where you see the best fit. This helps demonstrate confidence, but it also provides the listener with a direction and a target if they are able to help you. For example, "As a board director, I value businesses that are in a high growth phase. My experience scaling start-ups [company A and company B] would bring great value to an emerging firm that needs a strategic advisory board member to help it grow and scale while managing risk."

Personal Pitch Do's and Don'ts
Do

- → Show confidence in your language and purpose.
- → Start with a strong opener (that you have rehearsed) so you don't stumble over your words when asked, "Tell me about yourself."

- Speak calmly: Your communication style is being noted, and the people you are speaking to are imagining you on their board. If your elevator pitch is messy, disorganized, or flustered, they won't refer you for a board opportunity.
- Recite your pitch out loud so you can hear it. Test it on those you consider to be in your inner circle, and make sure you save the best version for the most influential people.
- Modify your pitch for the person you are speaking to.
- Make sure you are getting one or two primary messages across about your board ambitions during this pitch. For example, "I am seeking advisory board member roles in start-ups that need to scale an SaaS product."
- Be prepared to deliver your pitch in 30 seconds for the ultimate wow factor; practice your five-second elevator pitch as well. The first thing you say will determine if the listener wants to stick around to hear more.
- Maintain strong eye contact.
- Be authentic.

Don't

- Don't use too many "ums" and "ahs." They will take away from your ability to appear confident and professional.
- Don't speak too fast or too much, which is off-putting. Poise and articulation are essential when speaking to influential people. Plus, this will demonstrate your ability to communicate well when you are on a board.
- Avoid over-the-top language about yourself, like, "Let me tell you about my superpower" or "People say I am one of the best lawyers in Atlanta."
- Be serious, but personable. Don't laugh, be sarcastic, or try to be funny.

→ Speak naturally. Avoid memorizing your pitch such that it sounds over-rehearsed, delivered, or as if you are reading it.

Video yourself speaking out loud and watch to make sure you aren't using too many hand movements or touching your face or hair, and that you are making good eye contact. Review it as if you were speaking to yourself. What assumptions would you make about this person from the video? Do you exude confidence and self-assuredness? Are you speaking clearly and concisely? Consider asking friends and family how you come across.

Chapter 6 Summary

1. **Exude confidence:** Confidence is demonstrated by having a clear understanding of which boards you are best suited for and conveying your value proposition with a strong executive presence, meaning no stumbling or hesitation.

2. **Translate your expertise into board-relevant value:** Align your expertise into board-level responsibilities using words that demonstrate your understanding of what the board needs.

3. **Know your audience:** Appreciate the person or people you are speaking to by making your personal pitch relevant to them.

4. **Pitch format:** Follow a format that includes your overall brand, the three main things you will bring to a board, any board experience, and the type of board culture you believe fits best with your experience—all in under 30 seconds!

Section III

EXECUTION

CHAPTER 7

Networking Doesn't Have to Be Painful

"The world is full of people who are grabbing and self-seeking. So the rare individual who unselfishly tries to serve others has an enormous advantage."

—Dale Carnegie, author of
How to Win Friends and Influence People

When it comes to securing a board position, relationships are far more important than any resume or set of credentials you bring to the table. In fact, your reputation and your ability to build, cultivate, and leverage strategic relationships are often the key differentiators between those who land board roles and those who don't.

But many people consider "networking" to be a dirty word.

We surveyed more than a dozen senior executives who described networking as an arduous task of attending events with people they don't know. They also agreed that it felt awkward and desperate to speak to lots of strangers, and they disliked the idea of having to "sell themselves" after spending their entire careers building their credibility and expertise.

Further, these executives said that they did not like to ask their network for help or favors. None of them ever had to do this during their career. Their success always led naturally to new opportunities. Why would networking for a board search be any different?

Well, they're right! We would never recommend that senior executives who have built successful careers attend large networking events because they rarely lead to a corporate board seat. However, cultivating deeper, targeted connections with people who have influence in boardrooms will unlock board opportunities.

Tip #7: Relationships + Reputation = Trust Capital

Build the Right Relationships

Of course you have relationships! And you likely have a vast network of people you can reach out to. But the key is talking to the *right* people. That means spending 80% of your time re-engaging and rebuilding relationships with relevant existing contacts you haven't kept in close contact with based on the target boards you want to join and 20% of the time strategically building relationships with new contacts.

Why? Because people who like you and trust you will more likely refer you to an opportunity than someone you have just met. We're sure you have experienced this for yourself. Someone introduces you to a person who needs your help getting a job. You don't know them, but you take the call. But without knowing them, their work style, or their history, and without any personal experience, you are hesitant to introduce them to anyone or go above and beyond to help them. This is exactly what happens when you meet someone for the first time who could potentially help *you* obtain a board seat. If you think they will start moving mountains without the benefit of history or a personal relationship, you will probably be disappointed.

However, someone you worked with 20 years ago for five years and with whom you had a great relationship may be one of your biggest champions! Find out where they are today and set up a call to catch up.

Board member and former banking executive William "Bill" Jones said it best: "Your outreach needs to be intentional. It needs to be meaningful. Don't underestimate the power of your network; someone you know likely has a connection to someone you want to meet or to an organization seeking a board member."

Chapter 7 ■ Networking Doesn't Have to Be Painful

Focus your efforts on individuals who influence the board recruitment process or who have a high degree of influence with boards. This includes:

- **CEOs and other C-suite executives:** CEOs are usually the first to recognize the need for a new board member. Other C-suite executives, such as CFOs, COOs, and general counsel, are often aware of a new board member search or a desire to change up the board. Also, CEOs learn about board member recruitment efforts happening at other firms through their networks with fellow CEOs.

- **Current board chairs and nomination chairs:** The chair of a board or of a nomination committee is often heavily involved in the board recruitment process. Engaging with the chair allows you to gain valuable insights into potential new board member interest and expectations as well as trends in the industry. The chair, however, will not be operating alone; they will work with the CEO and possibly a board search consultant.

- **Executive search firms/search consultants:** These firms are often involved in recruiting for board positions. Establishing a relationship with them can give you early access to board vacancies and insider knowledge. An important caveat, though, is that the top executive search firms in the US cover the Russell 3000 (the 3,000 largest publicly traded US companies based on market capitalization) and, in some cases, the Fortune 1000 only (top 1,000 US firms by revenue). This is because search firms charge fees for their services, and not all companies have a budget for such high-profile searches. The same is true for nonprofit search firms. They only work with top-tier not-for-profits and often it is pro bono work.

- **Investors and shareholders:** Key investors and shareholders often have significant influence over board decisions and can help you understand what boards are looking for in new members. Private equity (PE) operating partners might be a good group of professionals to meet with if you are focused on PE firms because they may have oversight of their portfolio companies and board needs. Venture capital firms (VCs) tend to have their own team on the board of their investments, though it's common for VCs to have strong networks. Engaging with people you know in the VC space is always time well spent.

→ **Consultants:** Build a relationship with a company's corporate lawyers; they often represent boards and may see you as an asset in helping with corporate governance and advancing the business. Management consultants, investment bankers, M&A lawyers, and other consultants who work at the board and C-suite level will be privy to future board changes and any corporate actions taking place (e.g., IPOs or M&A transactions).

Find out if your network includes any of the people above. Do an advanced search on your current connections in LinkedIn using keywords on titles or industries. You will be surprised at who you may have forgotten about or who changed jobs in the last five years. Many former coworkers, bosses, investors, friends, or neighbors have joined a company or have a role that may interact closely with decision makers. Re-engaging with this group will be one of your best investments of time during the early stages of your corporate or nonprofit board search.

Another group of people who often get overlooked are the ones you sit with on nonprofit boards. If you sit on such a board, when was the last time you had a one-on-one meeting with any of the other board members? You may be surprised again at how well connected they are, and since they already serve on a board with you, they can speak to your skills.

We all have limited time, so while it's nice to reconnect with old colleagues and friends, be mindful of the people who won't be much help in providing you board opportunities. They may include the following:

→ **People with no influence:** Avoid individuals who have little or no influence in the board recruitment process at the companies of your choice. For example, if you are speaking to lots of operating partners of private equity firms but you want to join the board of a public company, you may want to adjust your strategy. Since they may not be able to help you move the needle, this will be time wasted. Of course, keep in touch if you'd like, but don't reach out with the expectation of advancing your board career.

→ **Highly competitive candidates:** When networking with people who are directly competing with you for board positions, tread carefully. These relationships may be less collaborative and more transactional.

Board Networking Strategy

Unlike typical career networking, which can often focus on immediate opportunities, board networking is about building long-term relationships that emphasize trust, governance acumen, and shared values. It's not about "selling" yourself but "positioning" yourself as someone who can offer strategic value to an organization. While traditional networking often involves meeting people to directly discuss job opportunities, board networking is more about creating organic conversations in an informal setting without any selling pressure to explore what you can bring.

In board relationship building, you'll often be speaking with executives, seasoned directors, and governance professionals. Your goal is to understand their experiences, get a sense of their needs, and see how you can help them. That's right! Helping them will help you! By delicately offering your own insights and positioning yourself as a valuable, future contributor to an organization's governance, you will help your contact see you from a board perspective.

Remember: Being on a board is not the same as being the CEO, CMO, CTO, or senior level executive. Your past senior leadership roles may have been in one particular department or industry. Your network may only know you from your previous positions.

Case Study

Geoff: Seeking a board position

Steve: Board chairman of one board and board director on many boards

Geoff is eager to gain a corporate board seat, so he messages Steve, someone Geoff has known professionally for eight years. Geoff hopes the meeting will result in Steve helping him find a board position. After all, Steve sits on various boards and is the chair of two of them.

Geoff's message reads:

> Hi Steve,
>
> I hope you are well.
>
> I have retired from [company name] and am now thinking about joining a board. Would you be open to a conversation to discuss my board career? I'd also like to hear about yours.
>
> Many thanks,
>
> Geoff

What Geoff doesn't know is that Steve frequently receives such requests from aspiring board members but doesn't always have time to accept all the meetings due to his busy schedule. Fortunately, Steve recalls that Geoff was a good client and is happy to take the call despite not having spoken to him in more than a year. They set up a Zoom call because Steve is in New York and Geoff is in Los Angeles.

Geoff prepares for the call by reviewing Steve's LinkedIn profile and checks out the websites of some of the boards he is on. As for preparing his own story, Geoff knows his career history and feels confident in knowing what to say.

Geoff writes down his goal for the meeting: to ask Steve if he knows of any available board seats and, if so, would Steve recommend him or keep him in mind for the future? Maybe Steve could also read his board bio and

Chapter 7 ▪ Networking Doesn't Have to Be Painful

give him feedback. He writes down a list of questions as well as a reminder to ask Steve what kinds of boards he thinks would be a good fit for Geoff.

The meeting starts and both Steve and Geoff arrive at Zoom on time. The meeting kicks off with some friendly catch-up but quickly moves onto the topic that Geoff is eager to discuss: his board career.

> As you know Steve, I retired from [company name] having spent 20 years there. I'm getting a little bored in retirement and my wife says I need to get out of the house! *(Geoff chuckles.)* So, I am currently looking at board opportunities at companies in the manufacturing industry where I have most of my experience.
>
> I suppose my first question is, what advice would you give someone like me on where to find such opportunities and how to start serving on boards? I have been talking to my network and I have a board bio. I think being on a board would be a good next step given that I have been a CEO and done a lot of M&A. I also ran our board at [company name], so I have a very good grasp of corporate governance.

Steve quickly realizes that Geoff is still in the discovery phase of the process and may need more time to put together a succinct value proposition. But Steve is polite, patient, and encouraging. He compliments Geoff on his experience and tries to be encouraging about how it could bring value to a board, even though Steve doesn't have nearly enough information to make that determination. He only worked with him in a business-to-business (B2B) partnership in the past and doesn't know enough about him. Steve quickly looked at Geoff's LinkedIn prior to the meeting but wasn't expecting to get this granular about his abilities to serve on a board.

Geoff asked all his questions about what kinds of boards Steve thought he would be good for and whether he would be considered for those types of boards. Then he realized that their meeting time was running out and he made the ask.

> Steve, if you hear of any board positions that would be a good fit for me, will you please let me know? And if I send you my board bio,

would you be willing to give me feedback on it? I want to make sure I have the right approach.

Steve replies, "Yes, of course. If I come across anything relevant, I will be sure to give you a call." And because Steve doesn't want to say no, he adds, "And, yes, send me your bio. I'll take a look and give you some feedback."

Geoff is smiling as he ends the call, thinking the meeting went great. He believes that Steve will look out for him and call him with a board position in the future! Geoff enjoyed reconnecting with Steve and was happy to hear so much positive affirmation about how he would make a great board member. He also looks forward to feedback on his board bio. Geoff believes he's made significant progress on his board career with this one phone call.

Steve, on the other hand, feels like the meeting was one-sided and a waste of time. He gained nothing from the interaction and now has agreed to review Geoff's board bio, which will take more of his time. Steve's board bio was created for him by a writer. His board positions came to him more organically, so he hasn't really used his bio that much. In addition, he doesn't even know what types of boards Geoff wants to serve on or the value he could bring. Steve decides he will do a quick read of the bio and send some comments to clear it from his to-do list. It was obvious to Steve that Geoff isn't ready for a board interview or even a board-level discussion. Once he sends off the bio and wishes Geoff luck on his search, Steve will return to his busy work schedule and forget about Geoff with no further thought.

Now let's look at the same meeting if it went a little differently.

Geoff: Seeking a board position

Steve: Board chairman of one board and board director on many boards

Geoff is eager to gain a corporate board seat, so he messages Steve, someone he has known for eight years, with the goal of proving that he is board-ready and actively pursuing a position. Geoff is eager to tell as many people as possible about his desire to join a corporate board. His message reads:

Chapter 7 ▪ Networking Doesn't Have to Be Painful

> Hi Steve,
>
> I hope you are well. It's been a while . . .
>
> I have retired from [company name] and I thought of you as we had spent so many years working together on business deals. Fun times back in New York City and London!
>
> Are you free for a friendly catch up on life and business next month? I'm sure you have a packed schedule, so let me know a few dates/times that work for you, and I will book a Zoom call for us.
>
> Many thanks,
>
> Geoff

Geoff prepares for the call and has notes on how the meeting will run and what he will say. He has spent hours preparing for this call because Steve is a person of influence and Geoff knows how important these types of people are in his board search.

Geoff opens the meeting by asking Steve how he's been and how he'd love to hear what Steve has been up to since they last spoke. While Steve gives his update, he mentions that he has been incredibly busy with a few high stakes business deals. Geoff did his research and hoped Steve would bring these up. He happens to know a lot about these companies and provides some insights. He also helps Steve think about some additional risks associated with the deal which Steve wasn't focused on. Once business talk starts to wane, Geoff asks Steve about his family. Steve mentions that he is taking them on a trip to Rhode Island next month. Geoff responds that he will send Steve the names of his favorite off-the-beaten-path restaurants from when he visited there last year with his wife. Steve is very appreciative of all the advice Geoff has offered.

Steve asks Geoff about his family and Geoff responds with a short account of how everyone is doing. Then Geoff transitions to his new goals:

> As you know, I retired from [company name] after twenty wonderful years and growing the business from a mere $1M to more than $800M. I am now actively pursuing corporate board seats.

Geoff notices on the screen how Steve's body language changes. He sees Steve lean in a bit as he responds.

> Wow, Geoff, that's great news, and as a board member myself, I can strongly recommend board service. What type of board opportunity are you looking for?

Geoff speaks confidently and concisely about his value proposition in growing companies, his experience in risk management and governance, what boards he is seeking, and who he is speaking to at the moment. Geoff connects the dots between his experience and the types of boards he believes he can bring the most value to. He knows Steve already trusts and likes him, so he feels no need to go overboard explaining his experience. Geoff knows his achievements speak for themselves.

Steve is impressed and instantly sees Geoff from a new perspective—not the Geoff he knew eight years ago as a CEO and business client. By hearing him speak about his previous experience from a board perspective and using board language, Steve believes that Geoff could come off well in a board interview and his mind is already thinking about which inquiries he's recently had where Geoff could benefit from an introduction.

Geoff finishes the meeting with,

> I'll send you my board bio so you have information on me as a potential board director.

Geoff never asks Steve to help him in this conversation, but Steve already wants to:

> Thank you, Geoff. I appreciate you sending me that. What a great meeting and I really enjoyed connecting. You know, there's another board chair I think you should speak to. He runs the board at [company name] and I know they'll be doing succession planning next year. My advice when you speak to him is to tell him exactly what you told me to see if there's a fit.

Geoff responds with his own action items:

Thanks, Steve. And I'll be introducing you to Will and Dana who can give you advice on some of the business questions you have. I'll also send you my own opinions on how to mitigate the risk for that business deal. Oh, and I won't forget to send you the names of some good restaurants in Rhode Island for your trip with your wife and kids next month.

They each have clear follow-up items and end the Zoom call.

Geoff is pleased with the outcome. He now has a referral from an influential board member. This is great progress. He also decides that he will check in with Steve every couple of months. And from their conversation, he knows that Steve often comes to New York, so Geoff will find out when his next trip is and perhaps connect in person. Steve is a relationship he needs to develop further for his future board career.

Steve is also pleased with the outcome of the meeting; he wasn't expecting anything other than a friendly catch-up with an old friend and client. He walked away with some relevant advice for his business and will also be getting some restaurant suggestions which will save him research time. In fact, Steve was so impressed with Geoff and his approach that he plans to not only introduce him to [company name] but he will spend some time thinking about who else he can introduce Geoff to. And he thinks that the next time he's in New York, he will reach out to Geoff to see if they can connect in person.

While the second case study clearly shows the better way to re-engage with previous relationships, why was the first one such a disaster? Let's break it down:

- Board-ready directors aren't desperate to get on a board or want to join a board because they are bored during their retirement.
- Board-ready directors don't *ask* people about the types of boards they should join; they *tell* them.
- Board-ready directors don't ask for help; they don't need it. They receive help because their contact will *want* to help them (without the ask).

- Board-ready directors don't need feedback on their bio; their bio is ready.
- Board-ready directors know their value and have confidence.
- Board-ready directors help others before expecting any help.
- Board-ready directors give advice on business problems or the industry/market to start proving their value.
- Board-ready directors speak clearly and concisely, the same way they would in a board meeting.

What else worked so well in the second case study that you can mirror?

- Asking your contact about *them* from either a business or personal perspective or both based on your previous relationship experience.
- Listening carefully for opportunities to offer advice, resources, and/or insights, adding value in the context of the conversation while trying to help them first.
- Being ready with a concise pitch on who you are as a potential board member, the value you would bring (using board language), and the types of boards where you would be successful. You don't have to prove anything—your value speaks for itself!
- Waiting for your contact to offer help, make introductions, or provide advice. If help isn't offered in the meeting, it may come later. One of Naomi's clients heard about a board opportunity from a contact eight months after networking call just like this one.
- Sending a follow-up email with your board bio and stating that you will touch base in a few months.

Follow up each meeting within 24–48 hours with a personalized thank-you note. Mention something specific from your conversation to show you value the connection. Over the next 6–12 months, stay engaged by sharing relevant articles, offering to help in some way, liking their LinkedIn posts/updates to keep you top of mind, or simply keeping them updated on your progress toward securing a board seat. From this example, if Steve introduces Geoff to potential board opportunities, Geoff will not only write a thank-you to those new contacts but also to Steve while keeping him informed on how those conversations went.

If you are someone who struggles to have these conversations, you now have a roadmap! Authenticity is key to these conversations, but that doesn't mean you can't follow a format. One of our favorite books, *How to Win Friends and Influence People* by Dale Carnegie, describes how to interact with people in social situations, especially when you want a desired outcome. As you take the next steps toward building your board career, we strongly recommend reading this book (again, perhaps) as you start re-engaging with old friends, coworkers, investors, and executives and cultivating new contacts at the highest level of influence.

When to Approach Others

Generating the right relationships is the single most important strategy for securing a board position, and it can't be transactional. It requires patience, genuine interest in others, and a long-term approach to building trust and credibility. Relationships take time to develop; getting started on this early shows you are thinking strategically about your future. Therefore, begin re-engaging old relationships or building new ones at least 12–18 months before you anticipate seeking a board role. And just because you want a board role doesn't mean one will be open when you are ready.

By strategic networking, nurturing relationships, and following through on the steps outlined in this book, you will position yourself as a top candidate when opportunities arise. The relationships you cultivate today will open the doors to your future boardroom success.

Chapter 7 Summary

1. **Cultivate the right relationships:** Spend 80% of your time re-engaging and rebuilding relationships with relevant existing contacts and 20% of the time building relationships with new contacts.

2. **Build a networking strategy:** Determine who you will talk to, when you will talk to them, and how you will create organic conversations (without any selling pressure) to explore how to help someone else and how they can potentially help you.

3. **Have patience:** Board hiring timelines vary by company, so be proactive in your networking while positioning yourself for a future opportunity that may not be on your immediate timeline.

CHAPTER

Board Preparation and the Interview Process

"Preparation turns a board interview from a pitch into a partnership conversation."

—Lesly Marban, private board director
and chief marketing officer

Boards engage in a formal interview process when there is a need for new board members. Such vacancies can arise due to retirement, expiring terms, resignation, or death, and boards typically act quickly to fill these roles to maintain governance stability. Vacancies can also happen during major organizational changes such as mergers, acquisitions, or leadership transitions that will trigger the need for a new perspective.

The majority of new board members at large US companies are brought on during or immediately following the annual shareholders meeting. This is because board elections and appointments are typically scheduled as part of these meetings, which are mandated by company bylaws and corporate governance practices. At these meetings, shareholders vote on board candidates and outgoing members rotate off as their terms expire, making this the conventional time for new board members to officially begin their terms.

Public companies usually start a search 9–12 months prior to the annual shareholder meeting, so staying focused year-round on meeting with the right people is essential because board vacancies show up throughout the year.

Tip #8: Forget what you know about job interviews. Board interviews are different.

That said, boards have also been known to recruit when there's a need for specialized expertise or a change in strategic direction or they simply find a great candidate who can bring value to the board and for whom they will create a position.

Tracking Board Openings

Here are some ways to track companies that may have board roles available:

- → **Public announcements:** Companies often make public announcements when a board member resigns or retires. These announcements can be found in press releases, 8-K filings (for public companies), or SEC filings.

- → **Investor relations:** For publicly traded companies, the investor relations section of their website or their press releases will often include information about board vacancies or new appointments.

- → **Board diversity reports:** Some organizations issue reports on their board composition, especially those companies that are required to publicly disclose diversity and governance practices. These may indicate upcoming changes such as when vacancies are anticipated due to retirement or term limits.

- → **Industry news:** Trade publications, industry reports, and financial news outlets will often cover high-profile changes to boards such as resignations, retirements, or the filling of a vacancy after a key member steps down. Monitoring relevant publications in your target industry will help you stay ahead of potential opportunities.

- → **Professional networks:** Many board appointments are announced informally before they become public. If you are networking with individuals in the industry, especially those in governance roles, they may share early insights or rumors about upcoming vacancies. Building relationships with board search consultants and even current board members will get you access to inside information.

→ **Board succession planning:** Some organizations may have publicly available succession plans, or they may share such information with investors or stakeholders during annual meetings or corporate updates. Tracking these plans will give you insight into when and how board seats turn over.

Board Interview Preparation

Preparing for a board interview is similar to prepping for a job interview: It requires deep research and diligent preparation. However, there are a number of key differences that set the board interview apart, so it's important to understand what is required of you, the candidate.

There are two basic foundational questions to be ready to answer:

1. Why you?
2. Why us?

Essentially, these questions are designed to find out why a company should add you to their board and why you are interested in joining their specific board. And while the questions are short, the answers are complex; it's all about what you can do for the board, not what you can get out of being a board member.

Describing your value proposition for a particular board is essential. One person who proved to be very good at this is Bill McNitt, a Chicago businessman who first sought out board roles in 2019. His clear and concise messaging made it easy for founders, CEOs, and other board members to see the value he would bring them, and he managed to join four boards in just 18 months! His advice? "You need to say what they want to hear, not just everything you want them to know about you. I was able to quickly describe what I would do for them. I focused on what *they* wanted and not just on my skills."

How did he know what they wanted? He did his research and asked powerful questions. He treated the interview like a sales meeting to understand their concerns and challenges and the direction the business wanted to go, and then provided them with a solution: him joining their board. But along with that solution must also come humbleness and respect for the leadership team and the other board members. Bill says, "You have to be careful not to appear that you are going to run everything and overstep your role." In short, you are not the savior but an important cog in the wheel.

The more research Bill did and the more he learned about each board, the easier it was for him to tailor which information about his experience and characteristics would be most relevant to his interviewers.

Board Research

Board research is much like the research you would do on a company for a job, but it needs to be deeper and more expansive. Here is a basic check list of areas to dig into (for certain companies, you may need to modify this list and/or seek additional research).

Public Company

- Read the most recent annual report and the most recent quarterly report.
- Listen to or read the transcripts of recent investor calls.
- Identify their top competitors and what they do differently. Determine what your target company is not doing that competitors are doing, giving the competitor's an advantage.
- Find the profiles of the leadership team; research their backgrounds and any potential connection you may have with them. And while this is extremely important to know, it would be premature and counterproductive to contact mutual relationships to discuss that connection and your board candidacy while you are in the initial interview process. Board searches are confidential, so leaking information to your contacts, friends, or other board members will be the fastest way to lose a potential board opportunity.

- Review the profiles of current board members. What specific skill or expertise do you offer that no one else has? Do you have specific industry knowledge?
- Conduct an online search. Start with [the company name] + board of directors + news and read everything that comes up.
- Research all social media platforms for recent posts. This will help you better understand the brand and the visible identity of the company and its employees.

Private Company
- Start with reading the website, as in *every page* of it!
- Do online research about the company to answer the following questions:
  - What is the company's purpose? Why do they do what they do?
  - What are the values of the business (especially family-owned or founder-owned).
  - Who are the investors? What is their track record?
  - Is it founder-owned, family-owned, private equity–owned, or venture capital–backed? Research the owners to understand the history of performance, leadership, etc.
  - What investment funding stage is it in?
  - What is the company's most important product or service?
  - Who is the company's target market?
  - Is it business-to-business or business-to-consumer or both?
  - How does the company make money? Can you find its revenue model?
  - Where does the company bring in the most revenue? Is it local, regional, international?
  - What is the largest expense on its profit-and-loss statement?

- Who is the chief executive officer and chief financial officer?
- Who are the other key executives, e.g., the chief strategy officer, chief technology officer, chief product officer, chief information officer, chief human resources officer?
- How many employees does it have?
- What has been its growth trajectory over the past five years?
- Is it currently holding steady or is the business scaling?
- Has it published a growth roadmap, sustainability goals, or M&A strategy?
- Is there any indication that the company is gearing up for acquisition or an IPO?
- Are there published DEI, environmental, social, and governance, or philanthropic efforts?
- Is it in a regulated industry (e.g., healthcare, financial technology)? What is its compliance history?
- Can you find anything about D&O insurance, whistleblower protections, or conflict-of-interest policies?

→ On LinkedIn, look at current and former employees to understand tenure and turnover. Look for testimonials or employee reviews on Glassdoor or Blind.

→ Research the company's competitors to understand how the company you want to join as a board member differentiates its products or services.

→ Research the board of directors: [company name] + board of directors + news.

→ Search for lawsuits or any legal disputes.

Employee Stock Ownership Plan

Unlike a traditional board, an employee stock ownership plan (ESOP) board is tightly connected to a fiduciary structure that exists to protect employee-owners' retirement assets. If an ESOP board interests you, do all the research you would do for a private company board and add the following:

- What is the history of the ESOP? Did it become an ESOP recently? If so, when and why?
- Are there repurchase obligations or valuation risks?
- How transparent is the company with ESOP participants (e.g., are there annual meetings or regular financial literacy sessions)?
- How is the company planning to fund the repurchase of shares? Is the obligation growing faster than revenue?
- Have there been recent changes to plan administration or trust strategy? Is the trustee internal or external?

Nonprofit Boards

- Read the website, as in (once again) *every page* of it!
- Answer the following questions:
  - What is the company's purpose and mission? Why do they do what they do?
  - What community do they serve?
  - What are their primary values?
  - Is it a local, regional, national, or international organization?
  - What is the history of the organization?
  - Who is its executive director? How long has that person been there?
  - Who are its sponsors or major donors and is there a connection between them?
  - What is the size of their endowments?
  - Is it a foundation? If so, which causes do they support?
  - What is the organization's largest expense?
  - How many employees does it have?
  - Has it been in the news for negative reasons?
- Research other nonprofits to understand how they are different.

- Does it have a board of directors and/or a board of trustees (or similar)? If so, what is the role of each?
- Does it have a "junior board" (a board of early career professionals who provide advice, fundraising, and advocacy for nonprofits they are passionate about)? If so, what do they do?
- Research board members: [nonprofit name] + board members + news.
- Search for lawsuits or any legal disputes.

Conducting early research on companies whose boards you would want to serve will help you know how to conduct quicker research later if a board search consultant reaches out to you for a position at a company that wasn't initially on your radar.

Board Search Consultants

The board interview process isn't all that different from the job interviewing process, but some board candidates are sourced through external executive search consultants (recruiters). That means companies contract with an outside agency to fill board positions. Some of the largest executive search firms have board divisions (known as the Board Practice), including Spencer Stuart, Heidrick & Struggles, Russell Reynolds Associates, Egon Zehnder and Korn/Ferry. This group is often referred to as "the SHREKs", because of the acronym of their names.

Board search consultants work on behalf of their client, the company, not you, the candidate. Their primary goal is to ensure the role is filled, regardless of who gets the offer, so they can get paid. While search consultants may make you feel great during the interview process, know that there is always more than one candidate being considered.

Every interaction with a board search consultant, no matter how minor, is an interview, so it's essential to make a strong first impression. Be prepared with your elevator pitch, dress the part, and ensure your bio, resume, and LinkedIn profile reflect your board readiness. Build a rapport with the search consultant so they become an advocate for your candidacy.

Jim O'Malley of the board and executive recruiting firm Kensington International had this suggestion for cultivating such rapport: Offer to help. For example, at the end of your conversation, ask the search consultant, "Are you working on any searches where I might be able to leverage my network to help you find the right candidate?" Consultants are always juggling multiple searches, and this small gesture makes you stand out.

The most important piece of advice? Be ready! If you connect with a search consultant before you are fully prepared, you risk missing out on the perfect board opportunity because they probably won't meet with you twice.

The Interview Process

Board consultants take their job very seriously. One bad board placement and the search consultant may lose that client forever. Therefore, they vet candidates thoroughly. Kerry Moynihan, a board search consultant who has been a partner and board member himself at firms including Korn/Ferry, Christian & Timbers, ZRG, Boyden, Desmond and Partners, as well a variety of NGOs and private companies, recalls interviewing a candidate who was a senior executive at a global company with revenue over $10B, and who served on a number of "prestigious" large public boards. But Kerry's rigorous due diligence surfaced a fraud allegation in which the candidate's company had been involved. Such an allegation or a perception of guilt is enough to torpedo a candidacy. Kerry was able to avoid a potentially embarrassing situation with his client by doing his homework.

While each board search consultant may have nuances in how they approach candidates, Kerry says the overall process is generally the same. Here are the basic steps and their order:

1. An organization's current board and executive team align on the skill set, diversity goals, and strategic needs for a new board member.
2. An executive search firm is hired to find a new board member.
3. The company educates the board search consultant about its board and what personal traits and experience would make for a great addition to the board.

4. The board search consultant should ask to sit in on board meeting(s) to better understand the culture and boardroom dynamics to help determine who will be a good fit.
5. With the help of the company, the search consultant will put together a detailed role description—a "spec"—that outlines the key attributes, responsibilities, and expectations for a board member hire. It serves as a guiding document for the search process and helps align stakeholders (board members, hiring executives, search consultants, and candidates).
6. The search consultant confirms the qualities, characteristics, and preferred traits for a new board member with the current board.
7. The search consultant begins the search, starting with referrals for potential board members from other board members and company executives.
8. The search consultant contacts potential board candidates discretely, providing information about the opportunity, including any potential remuneration for board service.
9. The search consultant conducts a preliminary screen with each candidate to ensure they possess baseline requirements, qualities, characteristics, and traits the company is looking for. If there is a potential fit, the search consultant will then ask a series of questions about the candidate's experience, background, and what they have/haven't seen in business and while serving on current or previous boards (if applicable).
10. The search consultant conducts thorough due diligence on each potential candidate, which includes verifying every statement on their board resume and bio.
11. For some companies, the search consultant will also conduct a deeper background check to ensure there are no hidden criminal or civil liabilities from the past.
12. The search consultant will seek references outside of those provided by the candidate to validate their ability to be a successful board member.

Chapter 8 ▪ Board Preparation and the Interview Process

13. The search consultant will create a standard board profile for each potential candidate to present to the client.
14. Client board members will decide who they want to interview.
15. Interviews with board candidates are scheduled.
16. The search consultant will review the interview results with the client.
17. The search consultant will review the results with each candidate and provide advice/guidance to those who will continue in the process.
18. Board candidates may have panel interviews, interviews with the CEO, CFO, and/or additional senior leadership executives—especially if they will be sitting on the executive board, and/or they may be asked to attend formal or informal dinners.
19. After each meeting and interview, the search consultant gathers feedback from the client.
20. The search consultant then provides feedback to the final candidates.
21. The company board makes its decision and informs the candidate(s) through the board search consultant or sometimes directly, that they have been invited to join the board or that their candidacy will not be moving forward.
22. There is typically very little room for negotiation on compensation when joining a board. All board members receive the same base fee. Chairs may receive an additional fee. Shares of equity may vary based on the company equity agreement and when you are asked to join the board.
23. The new board member will be given a legal agreement to sign.
24. Ideally, a formal onboarding process for the new board director begins with the company, though sometimes with the aid of the search consultant.

Not all board searches involve an executive search firm. In fact, the vast majority of candidates are found through networks, especially at smaller companies, family-owned businesses, and privately held companies. In these instances, the process can look more like this:

1. The current board and executive team align on the skill set, diversity goals, and strategic needs for a new board member. Sometimes this profile can change as the company leaders talk to more people. A "skills matrix" identifies gaps in subject matter expertise to ensure the board maintains a diverse and comprehensive set of skills.

2. The CEO decides not to use a search firm because of the fees (e.g., there may not be a budget allocated for such a search).

3. The CEO/CFO may ask the following people if they can help or if they know anyone worth speaking to:

    - Outside accountant or partner of an accounting firm
    - Their corporate attorney
    - Their investment banker
    - A well-connected friend on the golf course or at a membership-required club
    - Their mentor
    - Their spouse/partner
    - Investors or board members (However, the CEO may avoid these advisors if he or she does not already have a good rapport with them.)

4. Various people are introduced to the CEO. There may or may not be a board specification document. Most of the time, companies create one for formality, but some just start the conversation with trusted contacts.

5. The CEO has initial conversations with the candidates. These may appear to be informal, but don't be fooled: They are interviews! The CEO may present a problem the company is trying to solve to see how the candidate responds.
6. Candidates are introduced to the rest of the board. This may be in the form of one-on-one interviews or a panel interview with multiple people. Initial interviews are likely to be done on a digital platform such as Zoom. As candidates move through the process, subsequent interviews take place during in-person meetings.
7. Candidates may be invited to a dinner or informal get-together with other board members. This is another interview! But the conversations may be more informal.
8. The board will deliberate, and once a decision is reached, the CEO or main contact will extend an offer to the winning candidate and reject the other finalists.
9. The new board member will receive an agreement to sign and, in some cases, join the board immediately or at the next board meeting.
10. Onboarding can be in-depth or more surface-level. Either way, make sure to read Chapter 11 to find out what you need to know before starting a new board role.

The typical board search process varies depending on the company, industry, and urgency of the hire, but it generally takes four to nine months from search initiation to board appointment.

Types of Board Interviews

There is no specific "type" of interview. They can be virtual or in person, with one person or many, formal or informal. Keep in mind that whenever you are interacting with a current board member, you are in an interview.

Virtual

There are advantages and disadvantages to a virtual interview. Most board interviews will be conducted over a digital platform at least once, and you will often find yourself speaking to a board search consultant over a video call as well.

ADVANTAGES:

- → You can make notes and stay on point using them.
- → You may not be as nervous.
- → You can set up your background to make the best impression.

DISADVANTAGES:

- → Your audio or video may not be of good quality or set up correctly, which can affect the impression you leave.
- → The video call ends and there is no small talk. An in-person meeting might allow you to walk to the elevator with someone from the board and chat about additional items or connect in a more personal way.

In-Person

In-person interviews always provide an opportunity to connect on another level. You have a chance to shake the board members' hands, make close eye contact, and read their body language. You can make more of an impression with small talk before or after the interview. Further, when interviews happen at the company's headquarters, you may get a tour of the company and interact with some of the staff to get a better feel for the company culture.

Panel Interviews

This is where a group of board members (and sometimes a company executive) interview the candidate together. These interviews can be virtual or in-person, but such panels are generally held remotely because board members are often located in different cities. For nonprofit organizations, however, panels are more likely to be in-person as board members are local or regionally located.

Panel interviews could be your first interaction with the board or later in the interview process. While each board member will ask specific questions, you will be addressing all of them with your answers. Therefore, the more you know about each member, the easier it will be to address them individually and relate to their area of expertise.

The goal is to build a rapport with all the interviewers. And because having a group staring at you and firing off questions can be intimidating, practice maintaining eye contact with multiple people, say, at a dinner party while telling a story. This will help you connect with each panelist during the interview and not focus on just one or two people.

Most panels run 30–60 minutes depending on the group. It's okay to take notes during this meeting so you remember who asked which question. This will help you when sending thank-you notes to each interviewer, or the person who organized the meeting to pass along to the board members. And yes, you must send thank-you notes!

The 1-2-1 (one-to-one) Interview

A 1-2-1 interview is a private, face-to-face meeting between one interviewer and one board candidate where you can expect a deeper, more focused conversation. Compared to panel interviews, this may seem less intimidating, but even if the interviewer uses a more casual tone, it is not an invitation to let your guard down. He or she will still be intent on diving deeper into your experience, skills, and cultural fit.

Always follow the interviewer's lead and take note of cultural cues. Is the interviewer more extroverted or introverted? Are they talking fast or slow? Mirror their energy and cadence. Don't work too hard trying to talk about your agenda; let them direct the conversation.

When writing a thank-you note, consider referencing key points from your discussion and adding insights from your own experience. You might also include a thoughtful question similar to one that a board member might pose in a meeting. This approach highlights your strategic thinking and intellectual curiosity.

The Business Meal Interview

Many of our clients have had lunch, dinner, or coffee meetings as part of the interview process. This could be with the leadership team, the board, or both. It's hard to know what to talk about because of the informal environment, so here are a few recommendations:

- Be prepared to have more social conversations. This can include topics like your most recent vacation, hobbies, and your spouse or family. Such informalities give the board additional insights into your character and values.
- Be prepared to answer interview questions if they come up but don't delve too deeply into business unless you are asked to comment on a particular issue.
- Look at the restaurant, the time of day, and the company. Will there be a dress code, such as at a golf club? If you aren't sure, feel free to ask: "Tie or no tie?"
- Don't order messy food, food you eat with your hands (such as a sandwich), or food that will get stuck in your teeth (broccoli)!
- If everyone is ordering an alcoholic drink, consider how your body reacts to alcohol and what would be the least intoxicating to nurse during the meal. Drink slowly!
- Watch your table manners and how you treat the staff. They are watching your every move!

Some lunch or dinner interviews toward the final stages of the selection process may include your spouse or partner. This offers the board an opportunity to better understand you as a "whole person," including the support system around you. If you don't have a partner, that's absolutely fine. Just be prepared for the possibility of this kind of invitation and respond accordingly.

Top Questions to Prepare Answers For

There is no way to anticipate every question you may be asked. However, all answers in which an example is expected should follow the

STAR(T) framework: Situation, Task, Action, Result, and Takeaway. The added "T" encourages reflection beyond outcomes by highlighting what you learned, how you grew, or what you would do differently in the future. Done well, this helps showcase self-awareness, adaptability, and a continuous-learning mindset, making your response not just a story of success but a demonstration of personal and professional development.

Board questions that may lead to examples often address strategy, governance, risk management, growth, and transformation. They also care about influence, alignment, conflict, and communication. When you answer such questions, keep in mind how they fit into one or more of the three areas that boards focus on: oversight, insight, and foresight. Revisit the preferred board member attributes in Chapter 2 (advocate, collaborator, communicator) to ensure you are telling each story *as if you were a board member*. Bring all these qualities into the answers and stories you tell. Show the interviewer that you have insightful advice and will be an impactful board member.

Here are some examples of specific questions you may be asked along with guidance on how to focus your answers:

Governance and Leadership Experience

1. What motivated you to pursue a board position with us?

    GUIDANCE: Disclose what you will do for them and how the company's values align with yours.

2. How do you see your role as a board member differing from that of the executive team?

    GUIDANCE: Discuss how, as a leader and an executive, you are consistently executing large-scale strategy, and that as a board member, you would be focused on strategy, growth, managing risk, and providing oversight for transformation. This is a great opportunity to showcase your knowledge of governance and your fiduciary duty as an executive and how those responsibilities differ when becoming a board director (e.g., Duty of Care).

3. Can you share an experience where you had to provide oversight or strategic direction in a complex situation?

   GUIDANCE: Give an example as if you were already a board member and be mindful of the vocabulary you use. Emphasize your history of overseeing decisions and guiding teams versus doing the work and completing activities. Here's an example:

   "I recall one example when I was a senior leader in a company undergoing a major restructuring to pivot its business model. The situation was complex due to the need to balance short-term financial stability with long-term strategic goals, all while maintaining employee morale and ensuring shareholder confidence.

   "In my role, I provided oversight by working with the executive team to ensure that the restructuring plan aligned with our long-term vision. I provided strategic oversight including monitoring key performance indicators to help keep the restructuring efforts on track, and I regularly reviewed financial reports to assess the impact on our bottom line.

   "When there were challenges, such as resistance from certain departments or unexpected financial constraints, I guided the leadership team by helping them evaluate alternative approaches and consider the broader implications of each decision. I also made sure that communications with stakeholders, such as employees, investors, and customers, were clear and aligned with our strategic direction.

   "Ultimately, we successfully navigated the transition, stabilizing the business and positioning it for future growth. This experience refined my ability to step back and provide oversight from a strategic perspective while managing complexity and stakeholder expectations."

4. How would you handle a situation where you disagree with a majority of the board?

Chapter 8 ▪ Board Preparation and the Interview Process

GUIDANCE: Be aware that you will need to refer to personal stories when describing the process you went through to resolve the disagreement (assuming it was resolved), including who you spoke to, how you responded, what was said, and when it happened. (The wrong answer would be to say you've never experienced a disagreement, which doesn't sound authentic.) For example:

"In my professional experience, I've encountered situations where my perspective differed from the majority, and I've learned that the key to managing these disagreements is a balance of respect, communication, and data-driven decision-making.

"For instance, in a previous role, I was part of a leadership team deciding whether to approve a major investment in a new product line. Most of the team was in favor, but I had concerns about the financial risks and the market demand for the product. I didn't agree with their assessment, but I recognized that my role was to provide constructive input and ensure that the decision was made with the best interests of the company in mind.

"To support my concerns, I took the time to gather data and research market trends, competitor activity, and financial forecasts. I then approached a few board members individually to share my perspective, explaining my issues about potential financial implications and offering alternative solutions such as a phased investment approach or revisiting the product's market readiness.

"When the issue came up for the full board discussion, I made sure to clearly and respectfully present my views, backing them up with data. I acknowledged the majority's position but framed my disagreement as a concern for the long-term sustainability of the company rather than a rejection of their ideas. I also made it clear that I was open to further discussion and willing to consider additional information.

"Ultimately, the board decided to move forward with the investment, but my input led to implementing additional safeguards and

monitoring mechanisms. While I didn't win the argument, I was able to influence the final decision in a way that mitigated risk and helped the company move forward more cautiously.

"To summarize, when I disagree with the majority, I believe it's important to listen, respect others' perspectives, and present my views in a way that focuses on the organization's best interest. I strive to ensure that my disagreements are rooted in data and framed as a collaborative effort to strengthen the overall decision-making process rather than a challenge to the majority's views."

Financial and Risk Oversight

1. What is your experience with financial oversight and interpreting financial statements?

    GUIDANCE: If you have experience, explain it clearly. If you don't, describe different scenarios where you have had financial responsibilities (e.g., treasurer role on a nonprofit board or maintaining a budget within your team). Keep in mind that your answer should be clear about how you "interpreted" the financial data so remember to describe high-level business risks and opportunities.

2. How would you evaluate and mitigate risk at the board level?

    GUIDANCE: Describe the oversight you've had over a company's strategic plan and/or any experience on an audit or risk committee.

3. Have you ever navigated a financial crisis or restructuring? How did you approach it?

    GUIDANCE: Be mindful of language; use board language (governance) versus activities performed (operational) during the crisis or restructuring. Emphasize oversight and your ability to provide strategic direction.

4. What experience do you have with mergers, acquisitions, or divestitures?

GUIDANCE: Boards are looking for candidates who have been involved in all three stages of M&A: identification, negotiation, and integration. Where you can, describe your experience in each area even if you weren't directly involved but were at least in the room. Be aware that boards don't always want to hear the success stories, so be prepared to describe how an M&A transaction went sideways or when an acquisition didn't turn out to be profitable. That's where the "T" for Takeaway (from above) comes in. As long as you have grown and learned from the situation, you will show your ability to understand risks, see blind spots, and adapt.

Industry and Strategic Insight

1. What do you see as the biggest challenges, opportunities, and trends facing this industry?

   GUIDANCE: Research! Research! Research! You need to already know the challenges and opportunities facing the industry and the specific company for which you are interviewing for a board position.

2. How have you contributed to shaping a company's long-term strategy?

   GUIDANCE: Showcase that you have conducted market research and have access to knowledge about the industry that will be critical to overseeing strategic plans.

3. How do you approach balancing short-term performance with long-term growth?

   GUIDANCE: When answering this question, it's essential to demonstrate strategic thinking and an understanding of the broader business context. Respond with a clear understanding of both challenges and then explain how you would prioritize and align them. Highlight your decision-making framework such as in the following way:

"I use a multi-pronged approach. I review data and market research and I also rely on years of experience to assess the trade-offs between short-term and long-term decisions. For example, I evaluate both financial and operational key performance indicators to measure short-term performance and regularly review market trends and customer feedback to inform long-term strategies. By aligning these insights with the company's strategic vision, I ensure that decisions support both immediate needs and long-term objectives."

Be specific, demonstrate flexibility, and acknowledge the challenges. The goal, again, is to focus on the strategy of your approach.

4. Have you worked with regulatory bodies or overseen compliance in a heavily regulated industry?

   GUIDANCE: This may be an opportunity to describe your relationships in the industry as well as your experience. Don't forget that board members are brought on not just for their credibility but for their strong networks, especially when a company is seeking investment or preparing for an IPO.

Board Dynamics and Stakeholder Management

1. How would you build relationships with other board members?

   GUIDANCE: Describe how you would meet individually with each board member during the onboarding process. Tell them that you have attended board dinners prior to board meetings and gotten to know some of the members. This is also your chance to describe your style, values, and how you collaborate with others.

2. What is your experience with corporate governance best practices?

   GUIDANCE: The goal here is to demonstrate your understanding of governance principles and show how your experience aligns with these practices. If you have direct experience with corporate governance, this would be the time to elaborate on that. If not, you can still highlight transferable skills and relevant experiences that demonstrate your ability to oversee major initiatives. Start with defining corporate governance and its importance. Then, if you have experience, highlight it. If not, describe your application of transferable skills. For example:

"When leading the implementation of a new enterprise-wide software system at [company name], I worked closely with senior leadership to ensure that the project was managed transparently with clear accountability structures. We established regular updates to stakeholders, held management accountable for deliverables, and made sure the process adhered to both internal and external regulatory standards. Additionally, I ensured that risk management was a core focus throughout the project, regularly assessing potential risks and ensuring mitigation strategies were in place."

Conclude with how you will use governance best practices while on the board.

3. How do you stay informed about emerging governance trends and regulatory changes?

   GUIDANCE: Talk about your outside engagements such as sitting on the board of an industry association, favorite business news sources, and key members of your network. Discuss any recent courses you've taken on cybersecurity, automation, AI, quantum computing, and other emerging tools and technologies. You can also take this opportunity to showcase your knowledge of governance trends such as describing a conversation you had or a panel discussion you attended and what you learned.

Questions to Ask the Board

You must have questions! They should be strategic and provide for high-level conversation. The best questions will come from doing thorough research. And don't forget: Board directors ask questions that are useful, contribute to the success of others, are delivered in a respectful and diplomatic way, and leave biases at the door. In addition, board directors never try to prove that they are the smartest person in the room. Make sure your questions reflect how you would be asking questions in the boardroom while serving the stakeholders and shareholders!

Depending on what you have learned and what you want to learn before seeking to join a particular board, here are some questions to consider asking:

Company Growth Strategy

1. Can you walk me through the company's growth strategy and what role the board plays in shaping it?
2. What do you see as the biggest risks and challenges facing the company, and how is the board addressing them?
3. What transformational opportunities do you foresee for the company in the next 3–5 years?
4. What are the key assumptions behind the company's long-term strategy, and what would cause those assumptions to change?
5. Are there any major shifts or inflection points on the horizon where the board's involvement will be particularly critical?

Company Risk

1. Beyond the company's growth strategy, where do you see potential blind spots or internal challenges that could hinder its execution?
2. What major risks are not yet fully mitigated, and where does the board see potential gaps in risk oversight?
3. How has the board navigated a crisis or major industry shift in the past, and what lessons were learned?
4. How do you see the company's industry evolving, and what role does the board play in anticipating and preparing for those shifts?

Board Dynamics

1. How would you describe the cultural dynamics of this board—what makes it unique compared to others you've served on?

2. How does the board assess its own effectiveness, and when was the last time it did an assessment?
3. Are there any emerging or ad hoc committees that play a significant role in governance beyond the traditional ones?
4. How does the board typically interact with the leadership team and investors?
5. What do you believe makes a board member highly effective and valued in this specific environment?
6. How does the board support and challenge the executive team in a productive way?

Board Member Expectations

1. Are there any committees beyond the traditional ones that I should be aware of?
2. Are all board members expected to serve on committees?
3. How does the board determine committee assignments, and what factors influence leadership roles within committees?
4. What are the expectations for board members in terms of time commitment, committee involvement, and engagement?
5. Beyond the baseline time commitment, what situations might require additional time or engagement from board members?

Board Alignment

1. Can you share an example of a difficult decision the board had to make and how the board reached alignment?
2. How does the board balance short-term pressures from investors with its long-term strategic vision?
3. In closed-door discussions, what are the biggest areas of debate or contention among board members?
4. What are the key issues that the board will focus on this year?

5. Are there areas where the board wishes it had greater expertise or resources?
6. How does the board handle disagreements or differing opinions, and can you share an example of when alignment was difficult to achieve?
7. Was there a difficult decision the board had to recently make, and if so, how did that go?
8. What advice would you have for me as a new board member?

Nonprofit Board Questions

These additional questions are specific to nonprofit boards and should not be asked for any other board member positions:

1. What are the fundraising goals for this fiscal year and how is the board involved in achieving them?
2. Are there any emerging risks you see on the horizon that may impact your organization's ability to raise funds and serve your stakeholders?
3. Beyond the baseline time commitment, do board members participate in the organization's events?
4. Are board members expected to fundraise and/or volunteer their time outside of their board duties?
5. What is the organization's impact in the local and national community, and does it distinguish itself from the national organization?
6. Are there fundraising campaigns or initiatives currently in place or planned?
7. What role does the board play in being the public face of the organization, and how involved should I expect to be in public relations and advocacy?

Virtual Meetings: Do's and Don'ts

Some of these may seem obvious, but they still need to be said out loud!

Do's

- Make sure your background is professional and interesting—consider a nice painting, bookshelves with interesting books, or something else that could be a talking point. Make sure there are no messy shelves, crooked pictures, or clutter.
- Always be in a well-lit room. Never have a light or a window behind you; use a lamp or a light in front of you to light up your face.
- Watch out for glasses. They reflect the screen and the interviewer may not be able to see your eyes, or they will see what you are "reading" during your interview.
- Make sure your face is in the top one-third of the screen and that your shoulders are also in the picture.
- Your camera should be at eye level. Looking up or down at a camera is not recommended.
- Make sure your hair is appropriate, e.g., not in your eyes or covering your face.
- When in doubt about your workspace, use another desk or table that has the right lighting, background, etc. Since they should only be seeing you and not your desk, you don't have to interview at the space you work from.
- Practice how you will show up for the interview (e.g., the day before) and turn on your camera ahead of time to check that everything looks good.

Don'ts

- Never wave goodbye once a virtual meeting ends. It's a terrible last impression for a senior level board member to be remembered as waving their hand like they are saying goodbye to a loved one on a boat. Just nod and thank them for their time and smile while you click the Leave button.

- Don't have any dogs or other disturbances in the background. If you have pets, ask a neighbor or friend to take them for a few hours.
- Don't touch your hair, face, or eyes during the interview. Keep your hands below the screen if possible.
- Make sure you are alone in a room with the door closed. Being on a board is a confidential role! If you have a door open or there are people in the background, the interviewer will be uneasy about sharing information.
- Don't do a final practice 30 minutes before the interview. You don't want to sound too rehearsed.

Chapter 8 Summary

1. **Track board vacancies.** Keep a pulse on when boards announce vacancies through public announcements, investor relations emails and newsletters, board diversity reports, industry news, professional networks, and publicly announced board succession planning.
2. **Board interview preparation.** Preparing for a board interview requires deep research and diligent preparation.
3. **Leverage board search consultants.** Every interaction with a search consultant is an interview and a chance to build rapport with the consultant so they become an advocate for your board candidacy.
4. **Board interviews.** There is no way to anticipate every question you may be asked; however, all answers that ask for an example should be prepared in writing using the STAR(T) framework.
5. **Develop questions to ask the board.** You must have questions! They should be strategic and provide for high-level conversation.

CHAPTER

Goal Setting

"Understand that securing a board role is a marathon, not a sprint. Maintain persistence in your pursuit by always looking to make meaningful relationships while exercising patience in the process and don't be afraid to let people know of your aspirations."

—William "Bill" Jones, private company board director, former US Bank executive

Tip #9: SMART goals are a way to spotlight your intention and focus your action.

The best way to achieve any goal is to put it down on paper, but saying, "I want to join a board" isn't enough. Draft SMART goals (Specific, Measurable, Achievable, Relevant, and Time-bound) for getting on a board within a specific timeframe and break down your primary objective into actionable steps.

Define Your Primary Goal

Here is an example of how you can structure your SMART goals with a focus on the essential work required, such as networking, personal branding, and skill-building:

Step 1: Clarify Your Board Target

Think about the kind of board you want to join. Is it public or private? A small company, mid-sized, or large? For profit or nonprofit? Global, regional, or local? Also consider the type of industry where you can bring the most value. If you are chief financial officer at a medical technology company, it may be easier to join a med-tech board than, say, a financial technology company board, even though you have deep financial expertise. Set your overarching goal of exactly what you want and when you want it. For example:

> Secure a board position at a mid-size or large private company within 18 months, preferably with companies that are actively engaged in mergers and acquisitions.

Step 2: Break It Down Into SMART Goals

- **Specific.** Determine what needs to be accomplished and what steps need to be taken to achieve it.
- **Measurable.** Define your goal with quantifiable and trackable benchmarks so you know when you have reached it.
- **Achievable.** Your goal needs to be realistic and something you can reasonably accomplish.
- **Relevant.** Why is this goal important to you?
- **Time-bound.** Determine a reasonable timeframe to achieve your goal.

Here are some specific goals to consider that may be useful in your board search:

1. **Networking goal:** Spend five hours per month identifying and connecting with at least three experienced board members or influential professionals to build a targeted network of a minimum of 35 individuals over the next year.
2. **Board-specific skills goal:** Dedicate at least three hours a week over the next six months to taking and completing at least two courses or certification programs to enhance board-relevant skills (e.g., financial oversight).
3. **Personal brand goal:** Dedicate up to two hours a week for three months to develop a personal brand and consider

engaging a board coach for feedback to ensure all board materials (e.g., resume, bio, LinkedIn profile) and social media reflect a board-level brand.

4. **Research opportunities:** Over the course of a year, identify five companies or organizations per quarter and connect with someone from their board.

5. **Governance credibility goal:** Within the next twelve months, spend at least two days per quarter and up to five events engaging with governance circles through educational webinars or other networking opportunities to gain credibility and connect with board decision-makers.

Step 3: Monitor Progress and Adjust

→ Set up a monthly review to evaluate progress against your SMART goals.

→ Adjust targets or timelines based on what's working or where challenges arise.

About now, you are probably thinking this is a full-time job, and you already have a job! However, dreams are only dreams until you make them a reality. By following this structured approach, you create a roadmap for systematically working toward your goal of securing a board position. Each SMART goal is tied to actionable steps that, collectively, increase your visibility, credibility, and readiness to join a board within your desired timeframe. Writing them down as SMART goals will keep them top of mind and remind you of what you are trying to achieve; otherwise, it will simply become something you want to happen but likely won't make happen.

Create Motivation

Now that you have SMART goals, set yourself up for success with a list of who can help you reach your goals. As we've emphasized, you can't achieve a board position in a silo. You will need to network and rebuild relationships with potential allies. Take a few minutes to determine who can help you and why. This exercise will help you take the first step in achieving the goals you've set.

Who are the top five people I will speak to about my desire to join a board, and why them?

_____

_____

_____

_____

_____

Who are the second five people I will speak to about my desire to join a board, and why them?

_____

_____

_____

_____

_____

I will schedule my first networking call to tell someone I am actively seeking board roles by _____ [date].

I will have my first board interview by _____ [date].

Write these sentences and answers on a whiteboard by your desk or stick them on your refrigerator door. There is only one thing in the way of you getting on a board: Action! Taking action is the key to success.

Chapter 9 Summary

1. **Define your overarching goal:** What *exactly* do you want and when do you want it?

2. **Break it down into SMART goals:** Build goals which are Specific, Measurable, Achievable, Relevant, and Time Bound.

3. **Track your progress:** Set up a monthly review to evaluate progress against your SMART goals and then adjust targets or timelines based on what's working or where challenges arise.

4. **Create motivation:** With the busyness of our lives, it's important to give yourself motivation by identifying on paper who you will speak to, the value they can bring to your board search, and then making the call or sending the email!

CHAPTER

You Get a Board Offer— Now What?

"Boards don't want more information. They want insight."
—Ram Charan, business advisor and author of *Boards That Lead*

You've been offered a board position! Congratulations! But you can't just immediately accept. You will need to review the paperwork and ask questions before formally accepting a position.

Conflicts Check

Accepting a board position comes with fiduciary responsibilities, which include avoiding conflicts of interest. Before formally accepting, it's essential to conduct thorough due diligence on potential direct and indirect conflicts. The company will have likely already done this prior to offering you the position, but you need to be aware of any unexpected barriers.

Direct conflicts are those where your jobs or affiliations may have competing interests or shared customers. Indirect conflicts are subtler and harder to determine. These can come into play when confidential information from one role could inadvertently influence decisions in another.

In the case of public companies, they will ask you to fill out a lengthy assessment that will include disclosing all your stock holdings and investments. If you are unsure of how to answer the questions, you can always speak to the company's general counsel to get more clarity.

Tip #10: Ensure you've done your due diligence before accepting a board position.

If the organization is in a regulated industry, verify that your involvement will not create compliance or ethical concerns with your current (or a previous) employer. While it may be easy to simply ask your employer's legal department to approve your position on a board, the company won't know of your personal conflicts.

Here is a checklist to ensure you don't miss any potential conflicts:

1. Understand the Organization's Key Stakeholders

When evaluating a board offer, identifying key stakeholders is crucial for understanding the organization's ecosystem and ensuring there are no conflicts of interest. Stakeholders include anyone who has a vested interest in the organization such as customers, employees, suppliers, investors, regulators, and the broader community. Begin by researching who the organization serves, its primary customers or beneficiaries, and whether there are overlaps with your personal or professional commitments that could create competing interests.

The best place to look while exploring the organization's ecosystem is the company's annual reports, website, or stakeholder communications. This will help you identify customers, partners, and suppliers. Further, use industry reports, news articles, and regulatory filings to understand the organization's competitors and how they align with your existing commitments.

Next, look into the organization's investors and partners. Investors may have specific expectations or priorities that could influence board decisions. Partners, whether strategic or operational, might have relationships with competitors or other entities that you are affiliated with. Serving on the board of an organization that directly competes with one of your existing affiliations can create significant ethical and legal challenges. By analyzing these relationships upfront, you can ensure impartiality and fulfill your fiduciary duty without compromising your professional integrity.

2. Examine Your Existing Commitments

- **Review your current professional roles:** Begin by thoroughly examining your existing professional roles and affiliations, as these are the most common sources of potential conflicts of interest. Evaluate the organizations you work for, advise, or have financial interests in, and assess whether their operations overlap with the business of the prospective board. Overlaps can arise in several ways: shared customer bases, similar markets, or competitive products and services. For instance, if you currently consult for a company that partners with a direct competitor of the board's organization, this could create a conflict. Further, if you are interested in serving on a nonprofit board and you currently work for Pepsi, you may not be able to serve on that board if one of its board members works for Coca-Cola. Additionally, if you hold equity or financial interests in companies that operate in the same industry, these connections might influence, or appear to influence, your objectivity as a board member. Transparency about such interests is not only ethical but also vital for maintaining trust with the board.

- **Assess other board positions:** Serving on multiple boards can enrich your professional perspective, but it also introduces the risk of competing fiduciary duties. Fiduciary duties require that board members act in the best interests of the organization they serve, and conflicts can arise when two boards have overlapping priorities or competing strategies. For example, if you sit on the board of a supplier to the prospective organization, your decisions on either board could unintentionally favor one party over the other. Similarly, joining a board in the same sector as your current boards may increase the likelihood of sensitive information being improperly shared or leveraged. Before accepting a new position, carefully evaluate whether any potential conflicts are manageable, and be sure you can uphold your obligations to each organization independently.

→ **Consider family and close relationships:** While less obvious, these connections can still influence, or be perceived to influence, your impartiality on the board. For example, if a family member works for a competitor or owns a related business, this relationship could lead to questions about your ability to prioritize the interests of the board organization. Likewise, if a spouse or family member has significant financial investments in a competing company, this could raise concerns about divided loyalties. To address these risks, identify any such relationships early and disclose them to the board during the vetting process. Boards often have protocols to mitigate these issues, such as recusal from specific decisions, but proactive transparency is key to maintaining trust and avoiding reputational damage.

3. Analyze Financial Relationships

→ **Check for financial ties:** One of the most critical steps in evaluating a potential board position is to assess whether you or the company you work for has direct or indirect financial ties to the organization. Financial relationships can take many forms such as contracts, vendor agreements, or consulting engagements. For example, if your company supplies services to the prospective board's organization, this could create a conflict where your dual roles might influence or be perceived to influence the decisions made by the board. Additionally, consider any indirect ties, such as financial arrangements through third parties or partnerships where you might stand to gain financially. Even if such ties are minor, they can raise questions about your objectivity. Conducting a thorough review of your financial relationships ensures you are prepared to address any concerns transparently, preserving your credibility and fiduciary duty as a board member.

→ **Review stock ownership and investments:** Your personal investments and stock ownership also warrant careful scrutiny. Holding significant shares in a company that competes with or partners with the prospective organization could lead to perceived or actual conflicts of interest. For instance, if you own a substantial stake in a competing company, your decisions on the board might be viewed as favoring your financial interests over the organization's best interests. Similarly, investments in suppliers or clients of the organization could complicate your ability to make impartial decisions, particularly in negotiations or contractual matters. To mitigate these risks, identify any financial holdings that overlap with the organization's operations or strategic interests. If necessary, consider divesting from certain positions or disclosing your investments to the governance committee. Transparency and proactive conflict management will help you maintain integrity while serving on the board.

4. Understand the Board's Conflict of Interest Policy

→ **Request the policy:** Before accepting a board position, ask for the organization's conflict-of-interest policy. Most boards have formal guidelines that define what constitutes such a conflict and specify procedures for addressing such situations. These policies typically outline expectations for board members regarding financial interests, professional affiliations, and personal relationships that could impact their impartiality. By reviewing the policy, you gain clarity on the board's standards and any restrictions that might affect your role. For instance, some boards may have strict rules about serving on multiple boards in the same industry or engaging in certain financial transactions. Understanding these guidelines upfront allows you to assess whether your current commitments align with the organization's expectations and ensures compliance with the board's governance framework.

- **Discuss disclosure processes:** Proactively discussing the disclosure process with the organization is another essential step in managing conflicts. Confirm how potential conflicts should be reported and resolved, as transparency is a cornerstone of effective board governance. Most boards require members to submit annual disclosures detailing financial interests, affiliations, and relationships, but more immediate reporting may be necessary for evolving situations. Clarify whether disclosures are reviewed by a governance or audit committee and how the organization handles conflicts once identified, such as through recusal or other mitigation strategies. This conversation also provides an opportunity to signal your commitment to ethical governance and build trust with your fellow board members. Open communication about potential conflicts helps ensure that issues are addressed fairly and transparently, fostering a culture of accountability within the board.

5. Assess Compliance with Legal and Ethical Standards

- **Understand regulatory risks:** When joining a board, it's essential to familiarize yourself with the legal and regulatory framework governing the industry. Different sectors have unique legal obligations that board members must navigate, such as compliance with antitrust laws, Securities and Exchange Commission (SEC) rules, or industry-specific regulations that govern healthcare or financial oversight. For instance, if the organization operates in a highly regulated industry such as pharmaceuticals or banking, you could be held personally liable for breaches of compliance under certain circumstances. Similarly, roles in public companies require adherence to stringent SEC disclosure and reporting requirements. Researching these risks and seeking advice from legal counsel can help you determine whether you are adequately prepared to manage the regulatory challenges associated with the role. By understanding these obligations upfront, you can avoid inadvertent legal violations that could have serious personal and professional consequences.

→ **Consider reputational risks:** In addition to legal compliance, evaluate the potential reputational risks of serving on the board. Your association with an organization, particularly in a leadership capacity, ties your personal and professional brand to the company's actions. A history of unethical practices, poor governance, or ongoing legal challenges within the organization could reflect negatively on you, even if you were not directly involved in the issues. Research the organization's reputation by reviewing public records, media coverage, and stakeholder sentiment. Consider whether any past controversies or current risks might compromise your ability to uphold your own values or professional integrity. For instance, joining a board that has unresolved scandals could harm your relationships with peers, clients, or other organizations. By thoroughly assessing reputational risks, you can make an informed decision about whether the position aligns with your long-term goals and values and will protect your credibility.

6. Document and Disclose Potential Conflicts

→ **Prepare a disclosure statement:** Before officially joining a board, create a comprehensive disclosure statement detailing any actual or potential conflicts of interest. This document should cover all relevant financial interests, professional roles, personal relationships, and other affiliations that could influence your decision-making as a board member. Be thorough and proactive in identifying areas that might appear to be conflicts, even if you believe they are unlikely to create actual issues. For example, disclose equity stakes in companies within the same industry, consulting engagements, or any familial ties to individuals with connections to the organization. By providing this information in a clear, organized format, you demonstrate your commitment to transparency and ethical governance. This proactive approach helps the board identify and address potential concerns and sets the stage for a relationship built on trust and accountability.

- **Meet with the board chair or governance committee:** Once you've prepared your disclosure statement, schedule a conversation with the board chair or governance committee to discuss your findings. This is an opportunity to address any ambiguities or complexities in your disclosures and seek guidance on how the board handles potential conflicts. By engaging in this conversation early, you signal your willingness to collaborate on solutions and prioritize for the organization's best interests. Furthermore, initiating this dialogue builds credibility with the board, demonstrating that you take your fiduciary responsibilities seriously. Transparency at this stage not only ensures proper handling of potential conflicts but also establishes a strong foundation for your role as a trusted and effective board member.

Board Contract

When you accept a board position, you will be presented with a contract which will have specific terms for your participation. When reviewing it, make sure you understand and agree with the terms of your service. You can also have an attorney review the agreement. Here are some key areas to evaluate:

- **Responsibilities and expectations:** Review the Responsibilities section and confirm that the contract addresses your participation in meetings, committee assignments, and required time commitments. The language should state you are not responsible for day-to-day activities or the operations of the company, and you will not be required to supervise any of its business or affairs. Therefore, you will be designated as an independent contractor.

- **Service time:** Review the length of your term and whether it's renewable or has a term limit. Your service time, whether it's one year, two years, or open-ended, should be stated clearly, with a mutual ability to terminate the relationship at any time for any reason (or for no reason), with or without prior notice. Review the contract for any additional obligations such as fundraising, advocacy, or mentoring activities.

→ **Fiduciary duty:** Look for language that explicitly defines your fiduciary responsibilities, such as the duty of care, loyalty, and obedience, and make sure you understand your obligations.

→ **Indemnity clause:** Make sure the contract includes indemnification provisions that protect you from personal liability for decisions made in good faith as a board member.

→ **Director and officer (D&O) insurance:** Verify that the organization provides D&O insurance coverage, and review the policy limits and exclusions to ensure sufficient protection.

→ **Legal representation:** Review the contract to determine if the organization will provide legal representation in the case of lawsuits or regulatory investigations.

→ **Compensation and benefits:** If the role is compensated, review the details on stipends, stock options, or other benefits. Confirm payment terms and whether they align with industry standards. On the majority of boards, all board members in the same roles are paid the same. However, don't be shy about asking whether you are receiving the same compensation and benefits as other board directors because the chairman, certain committee members, and/or earlier board members may have different agreements. Finally, look for a reimbursement policy to confirm that expenses for travel, lodging, or professional development related to board service are reimbursed.

→ **Conflicts:** After you've done your research on any potential conflicts, review the guidance on disclosing and managing conflicts of interest, including the process for recusal from decisions.

→ **Confidentiality:** Review the requirements for maintaining the confidentiality of sensitive organizational information, including after your term ends.

- **Governance and decision-making:** Clarify your voting rights and any limitations, especially if you're serving on an advisory or nonvoting board. Further, verify that the contract references key governance documents, such as bylaws and charters, to understand the rules guiding board operations.

- **Regulatory compliance:** Compliance obligation clauses should clearly articulate your duty to adhere to all legal, regulatory, and ethical standards relevant to the organization's industry. For example, sectors such as healthcare, finance, or technology often involve specific regulations that board members must navigate to avoid liability or reputational risks.

- **Dispute resolution:** Identify how disputes between you and the organization will be resolved, including whether arbitration or mediation is required.

- **Post-service obligations:** Check for unreasonable restrictions on your future activities after leaving the board such as restrictive noncompete agreements or nonsolicitation clauses. Also, take note of any obligations to maintain confidentiality about the organization's information after your service ends.

By thoroughly reviewing these elements and seeking legal advice, if needed, you can make an informed decision about joining the board and protect your interests while fulfilling your duties effectively.

Questions to Ask

If you are unclear on any of the above, ask questions to fully understand the commitment you are making. This includes time commitments for meetings, preparation, and additional duties like special projects, as well as performance expectations, including specific benchmarks or outcomes expected of board members during your term and what committees you may be considered for. Consider phrasing such as:

Chapter 10 • You Get a Board Offer—Now What?

1. What is the expected time commitment, including meetings, preparation, and additional duties, such as committee work or special projects?
2. Are there any specific benchmarks or outcomes expected of board members during their term?
3. What committees will I be considered for?

Additionally, find out if there is any training that might cover governance best practices, industry-specific regulatory compliance requirements, or emerging trends affecting the organization. If the organization provides such training, it is demonstrating a commitment to equipping its board members with the knowledge and tools necessary to perform their duties effectively and in alignment with applicable standards. To explore these opportunities, ask the following:

1. Are there specific regulatory risks or legal obligations I should be aware of in this role?
2. Are there mandatory or optional training sessions and, if so, who bears the cost of these?

Ensure you understand your voting rights and what committees you may be asked to join through thoughtful questions expressing your interest:

1. Do I have full voting rights, and are there any limitations on my ability to participate in decisions?
2. Are there specific committees you think would be a good fit for me or that you would expect me to join, and what are their responsibilities?

Finally, you will want to understand if there are any restrictions after you leave the board. You don't want to be surprised later! Some easy questions to consider:

1. Are there any restrictions on my activities or affiliations after I leave the board?
2. What are my obligations regarding confidentiality once my term ends?

By asking these questions, you will address any ambiguities, identify potential risks, and ensure that the terms of the agreement align with your expectations and professional goals. Consult with legal or financial advisors to review the contract and provide guidance on any area you may not be familiar with.

Chapter 10 Summary

1. **Conflicts check:** Before formally accepting, companies will conduct thorough due diligence on potential direct and indirect conflicts, so make sure you are all clear before you move forward with next steps.
2. **Review the board contract:** Understand the terms of your service on the board and consider having an attorney review the agreement.
3. **Ask questions:** Determine if you need more information on any areas before signing, including time commitments for meetings, preparation, and additional duties, like special projects, as well as performance expectations, such as specific benchmarks or outcomes.

CHAPTER

The First 90 Days

"Jump in with curiosity, listen with humility, contribute with clarity. That's how you earn your seat and your say."

—Alison Levin, private company board director, nonprofit board chair, and president, NBCUniversal Advertising & Partnerships

Tip #11: Understand the business, the boardroom dynamics, and how to contribute with precision.

You Made It—Now the Real Work Begins

Landing a board seat is a significant achievement, but your effectiveness and reputation will be shaped by what you do in the first 90 days. This chapter is about shifting from "getting the seat" to earning your voice at the table.

Here are the top three strategies to help you start strong and build influence from day one:

1. Do Your Research

Before onboarding, do your homework. Review prior board packets, annual reports, financial statements, and relevant industry commentary to understand the organization's history, challenges, and strategic direction. This background equips you to ask smarter questions and avoid missteps early on. By showing that you're here to learn before leading, you signal humility, seriousness, and commitment, which are qualities that build trust with fellow board members far more effectively than *trying* to impress. When directors demonstrate genuine interest in the company's long-term success, their contributions carry more weight and credibility.

2. Shift Your Mind from Management to Oversight

If this is your first board experience, it may take a moment to shift your thinking from execution to oversight. Successful board members operate with a "nose in, fingers out" approach: They provide strategic guidance while allowing the CEO to run the company, avoiding micromanagement.

3. Observe Boardroom Dynamics

In your initial meetings, you may begin to sense subtle (or not-so-subtle) tensions between board members or between the board and organizational leadership. These dynamics can be rooted in a range of issues: prior strategic disagreements, clashing communication styles, diverging visions for the organization, or even unresolved personal or family conflicts, particularly in founder-led or family-owned businesses, where emotions and history may run deep.

Rather than jump to conclusions, it's critical to *read the room with curiosity, not judgment.* Avoid making assumptions about individuals based on limited interactions or hearsay. Body language, tone of voice, who speaks when (and who doesn't), and how people respond to dissent can tell you far more than formal bios or organizational charts. Ask yourself: Who holds influence? Who tends to defer? Where is trust strong and where is it missing?

Boardroom culture isn't always obvious on day one, but it begins to reveal itself through small moments: side comments, how conflict is managed, whether tough questions are welcomed or sidestepped. These observations are essential for shaping how you show up. As a new board member, your early posture should balance confidence with humility, so be engaged but also listen more than you speak.

Even in your first 90 days, you are responsible for contributing to a collaborative and effective board culture. That doesn't mean solving long-standing issues overnight, but it *does* mean paying close attention to interpersonal undercurrents, building relationships intentionally, and modeling curiosity and respect. Over time, your presence and approach can help ease tensions, bridge divides, and elevate the quality of board decision-making.

4. Be Strategic with Your Voice

You were chosen for a reason, so feel free to leverage your experience, judgment, and perspective. But remember: Effective communication on a board is about quality, not quantity. Resist the urge to speak frequently just to establish credibility. Instead, make thoughtful, well-timed contributions that build on others' ideas or introduce new dimensions to the discussion. Sandra Helton, a public company board member, comments, "Unless it is urgent, first-time board members should take the time to listen and observe during their first board meetings." Strategic input is valued over dominance, and patience often leads to more impactful decisions. Further, active listening and asking clarifying questions signal emotional intelligence and governance maturity. You'll be remembered for what you add, not how often you speak.

5. Build Relationships

Board service is a long game built on relationships. Invest time in getting to know each of your fellow board members outside of formal meetings. A premeeting coffee, a follow-up email, or a genuine compliment on a colleague's insight can go a long way. Build a strong relationship with the board chair and the CEO to understand expectations and deepen trust. People advocate for those they know and respect. Influence begins with connection.

6. Be Collaborative

Success in the boardroom is not about personal recognition; it's about collective wisdom. The most respected board members elevate others, build bridges, and contribute to a shared vision. Collaboration, diplomacy, and discretion are critical. Healthy debate is productive; "gotcha" questions and one-upmanship are not. Strong boards foster mutual respect and psychological safety, ensuring every voice is heard even when opinions differ.

Collaboration also means balancing confidence with humility. Bring your expertise to the table, but know when to speak and when to listen. Integrity is essential. Trust, fairness, and ethical conduct underpin everything a board does. Upholding your fiduciary duties, including the Duty of Care, Duty of Loyalty, and Duty of Obedience, requires discretion, confidentiality, and a commitment to the organization's greater good over personal gain.

7. Prepare for Every Interaction

Preparation is another pillar of board excellence. As Sandra Helton advises, "Be prepared before board meetings to ensure you can contribute in a meaningful way from the start." That means reviewing all materials in advance, identifying key risks and opportunities, and being ready with insightful, nonadversarial questions. The best board members challenge constructively, ask the hard questions—and the right questions—to surface important issues, and sometimes choose silence when it's the more strategic move.

Onboarding

Most boards have a formal onboarding process, but some are better at it than others. Again, according to Helton, one particular public company gave her a manual that consisted of all the information new board members needed to get started. This was one of the most organized transitions she had ever experienced. A great onboarding experience is important.

Bill Jones, who serves on both private company and nonprofit boards, has had the exact opposite experience where formalized onboarding for new directors was nonexistent. He recognized immediately that "this is not a good way to start," adding that the absence of onboarding showed "a lack of appreciation for good corporate governance." He says his time on that board started poorly until he created his own manual, and that, once onboarded, he worked to change that experience for future board members. On the flip side, another board he served on used a thorough *Board of Directors Handbook* as the agenda for an all-day onboarding session. Every experience can be different, so be prepared for the worst and hope for the best!

Therefore, develop a list of items and reports you expect for your onboarding, and if you don't receive this information, consider a conversation with the chair. Just in case you don't know what to ask for, no worries, we did it for you! Keep in mind that the list below may change depending on the type of board you are joining. The items will be most relevant for a public or private company board. (If it's a public company board, you may be able to access some of this information from public filings.) Nonprofit organizations should also provide a detailed report.

Company Information
- Analyst reports for the past year
- Company charter and bylaws
- Company code of business conduct and ethics
- A list of key investors along with insights on their perspectives of the company and summaries of feedback from investor engagement
- Executive incentive plans (e.g., annual, long-term)
- Financial reports including the annual report, budgets, and projections
- Investor presentations from the past year
- Key customers, opportunities, and vulnerabilities
- Organization chart
- Past earnings releases
- Regulatory, legal, and governance issues
- Results of recent employee surveys

- Strategic plans
- Stock ownership expectations
- Travel, expense reimbursement, and other policies
- Business model, key performance indicators, and profitability history with a review of both past performance for context purposes, current objectives and projections, and long-range plans
- Industry insights including trends, comparisons, key competitors, and potential disruptors
- Operational challenges and underlying infrastructure

Board Information

- Board and committee calendars
- Board committee charters
- Board corporate governance guidelines
- Board portal (if there is one): secured technology that holds board notes
- How meetings are conducted
- Capital strategies, resources, and covenants including lines of credit and longer-term credit facilities
- Committee assignments, roles, and responsibilities
- Directors and officers insurance policy
- Director profiles and contact information
- Prior 12 months' board materials and minutes
- Risk profile, including how the board views sector and company risk and how management assesses, presents, and articulates risk
- Most recent board evaluation
- Most recent committee evaluations (with appropriate committee chair)

- Board/committee activities over the previous 12 months of meetings
- Most recent CEO evaluation (with appropriate independent board leader or committee chair)
- CEO succession plan (with appropriate independent board leader or committee chair)
- Board-specific "nuts and bolts" (e.g., voting rules)
- Director roles and responsibilities (key for first-time directors)
- Transcripts or recordings of quarterly investor calls, if not accessible on company website

One-on-One Meetings

As you gather information for your own onboarding, schedule one-on-one meetings/calls with all current board directors, prioritizing the independent chair or the lead independent director and the chair of each board committee. Ask if you can attend all committee meetings for at least the first six months of board service to understand the nuances of what is happening in each committee. Plan a site visit and schedule meetings with key business executives and functional leaders including engineering, finance, marketing, IT, HR, legal, IR, internal audit, and any other key areas. Finally, schedule one-on-one meetings with external advisers such as accountants, compensation consultants, and any outside counsel to introduce yourself. As you build relationships and find synergies with specific board members, ask one or two of them to mentor/coach you, share feedback, provide perspective on boardroom activities and dynamics, and act as a sounding board between meetings.

Joining a board is an exciting new chapter that asks you to shift from operational execution to strategic thinking, from managing teams to governing enterprises, from day-to-day problem-solving to long-term value creation. It can feel exhilarating, even a bit daunting. But you're not on the board by accident. You're there because your perspective matters. Now's the time to lean in, listen deeply, and lead with intention. Believe in your positive impact . . . starting now!

Chapter 11 Summary

1. **Earning your voice at the table:** Shift your mindset to onboarding. Be curious, strategic, collaborative, and prepared for every meeting.

2. **Onboarding research:** Create a checklist of documents to obtain, research to do, and market information to obtain and absorb so you are prepared to join a board that is already "in progress."

3. **Onboarding meetings:** Set up meetings with the other board members, company executives, and external advisors to build relationships, and seek out a mentor who can provide you with feedback on your interactions in board meetings and help you adjust.

About the Authors

Naomi Kent is a strategic advisor and mentor to senior professionals who want to build a corporate board career. She spent nearly 13 years with BoardEx, one of the largest private providers of board and senior executive intelligence in the world, where she interacted with consultants and businesses that engage with all types of boards. While at BoardEx, she saw firsthand how boards operate, how individuals build board careers, and how referrals and references are made for board candidates, gaining a unique insight into the ecosystem of how boards recruit. Naomi is a trusted partner to the C-suite, senior professionals, and board members, a strategic advisor to those seeking board seats, and a motivating force behind positive career change.

For advice on building your board career, reach out to Naomi at **www.theboardroomco.com** and follow her on social media:

Linked In   **Instagram**   **YouTube**

To listen to Naomi's podcast, "The Boardroom Company Live," scan here:

Marlo Lyons is an award-winning, best-selling author, podcast host of "Work Unscripted," a licensed attorney and globally certified executive, team, and career coach. She has successfully worked as an executive across multiple industries and organizations from start-ups to Fortune 100 companies. Marlo has also served as a board director for a nonprofit in Los Angeles and works as a strategic advisor to board directors and as an executive coach to C-suite executives and their senior teams. Her direct experience in legal risk management, crisis communications, human capital strategies, and organizational transformation, combined with her expertise in career transitions, interviewing, and brand positioning, make her a sought-after executive coach.

For executive, team, or career coaching to advance your career and build a board career, reach out to Marlo at **www.marlolyonscoaching.com** and follow her on social media:

Linked In **Instagram** **YouTube**

To listen to her podcast, "Work Unscripted," scan here:

Notes

Introduction

1. https://www.lodestoneglobal.com/_files/ugd/c3325c_3c737aee44de4f2d93b164a6d2804604.pdf.

Chapter 1

1. https://www.lodestoneglobal.com/_files/ugd/c3325c_3c737aee44de4f2d93b164a6d2804604.pdf.
2. Marlo Lyons, *Wanted → A New Career: The Definitive Playbook for Transitioning to a New Career or Finding Your Dream Job* (Future Forward Publishing, 2022). https://www.amazon.com/dp/1737018128/?bestFormat=true&k=wanted%20a%20new%20career&ref_=nb_sb_ss_w_scx-ent-pd-bk-d_k0_1_19_de&crid=U1QD8DRRUZRW&sprefix=wanted%20a%20new%20career.

Chapter 2

1. https://www.govinfo.gov/content/pkg/COMPS-1883/pdf/COMPS-1883.pdf.
2. Dennis J. Cagan, *The Board of Directors for Private Enterprise.* https://www.amazon.com/Board-Directors-Private-Enterprise/dp/1524660159.

Chapter 3

1. https://boardex.com/; https://www.dnb.com; https://directormoves.substack.com/about; https://www.zoominfo.com; https://get.pitchbook.com; https://www.factset.com/; https://www.bloomberg.com.

Chapter 4

1. www.directorsandboards.com.

Index

About section (LinkedIn profile), 92–93
Academic and research boards, 38–39
Advisory boards
   board attire choice, 87, 90
   corporate, 37–38
   requirements for applying, 83
   scientific, 38
   start-up/large public, 42, 43
   strategic, 103
Agenda setting, 58
AI (artificial intelligence) programs, 15, 77
Antitrust laws, 162
Ariel Investments, 73
Attributes of board members, 26–30
   collaboration, 1, 11, 17–18, 27–28, 55, 61, 64, 102, 113, 144
   commitment, 10–11, 13, 28–31, 40, 46–48, 147–148, 158–159, 162
   curiosity, 29, 176
   diplomacy, 27, 172
   effective communication, 28–29, 65, 171
   engagement, 9, 12, 17, 28–29, 40, 54, 68, 76–77, 147
   ethical leadership, 27–28, 162, 163
   independence, 29, 72
   integrity, 15, 18, 27, 159, 161, 163, 172
   passionate advocacy, 29–30
   practical visionary, 29

   strategic thinking, 21, 26–27, 26–28, 41, 137, 143, 175
   strong governance knowledge, 27
   subject matter expertise, 27, 84, 86, 93, 100, 134
Audit committee, 23, 58
Authenticity (value string), 16, 18

Biography (bio), 3, 82–84, 114–116, 120, 130, 132
BlueSky, 75
Board choice, 33–49
   academic/research boards, 38–39
   advisory boards, 37–38
   corporate boards, 34–35
   fund boards, 39–41
   nonprofit boards, 35–37
   public sector boards, 38
Board choice, steps in choosing, 40–48
   check box, 40–41
   database background searches, 45–46
   due diligence tips, 46–48
   experience assessment, 41–43, 45
   targeting check boxes, 43–44
   values assessment/alignment, 40–41
Board committees
   audit, 22, 58, 85, 88, 93, 101, 142, 162
   compensation, 22, 71, 73, 85
   corporate social responsibility (CSR), 60

Board committees (*continued*)
  description, 70
  fundraising, 88
  governance, 23, 64, 74, 161–162, 164
  investment, 88
  municipal planning, 38
  nomination, 11, 14, 71, 74, 93, 111
  risk, 23, 62, 85, 142
  technology, 93
Board contracts, key areas, 164–166
  compensation and benefits, 165
  conflicts, 165
  conflicts/confidentiality, 165
  director and officer insurance, 165
  dispute resolution, 166
  fiduciary duty/indemnity clause, 165
  governance/decision-making, 166
  legal representation, 165
  post-service obligations, 166
  regulatory compliance, 166
  responsibilities/expectations, 164
  service time, 164–165
Board documents
  biography (bio), 3, 82–84, 114–116, 120, 130, 132
  resume, 53, 57, 83–87, 109, 130, 132
Board interlocks, 70
Board-level language, 57–75
  agenda setting, 58
  audit committee, 23, 58
  board committees, 70
  board evaluation, 70
  board interlocks, 70
  board refreshment, 71
  change management, 59
  compensation committee, 22, 71
  compliance, 59

conflict of interest, 59, 70, 161–162
consensus building, 59
corporate social responsibility, 58, 60
crisis management, 10, 23, 60
critical decision-making, 12, 60
cross-functional collaboration, 61
cybersecurity oversight, 61
director independence, 34, 39, 72, 74, 175
director liability, 72
directors and officers (D&O) insurance, 72
enterprise risk management, 62
environmental, social, and governance, 3, 58, 62, 128
equity compensation, 13, 73
ethical oversight, 62
executive leadership team, 9, 14, 56, 63
executive sessions, 73
fiduciary duty, 63, 72, 138, 159–160, 165
financial acumen, 40, 63
financial oversight, 10, 64, 94, 142, 152, 162
global perspective, 64
governance, 64–65
human capital, 27, 65, 94
influence, 65
innovative leadership, 66
materiality, 66
mergers and acquisitions, 34, 54, 66, 152
nomination process, 74
onboarding, 74, 133, 135, 144, 172–175
overboarded, 175
oversight, 67

Index

profit and loss (P&L) responsibility, 67
proxy statement, 67
regulatory knowledge, 67
risk appetite, 23, 68
risk management, 68
shareholder activism, 68
stakeholder engagement/alignment, 68
stakeholder resolutions, 69
strategic oversight, 41, 55, 69, 86, 95
succession planning, 35, 69, 125
transformation, 69
Board materials, 81–96
  biography (bio), 3, 82–84, 114–116, 120, 130, 132
  LinkedIn profile, 87–95
  resume, 53, 57, 83–87, 84–86, 109, 130, 132
Board members/membership
  attributes of, 26–30
  choosing a board, 33–49
  decision-making process, 23
  emails about joining, 1
  identifying/defining personal values, 14–19
  mistakes made by, 26
  motivation for joining, 8–14
  qualities sought by boards, 2
  relationship-building with, 111
  representation of women, 2
  responsibility to stay informed, 25–26
  risk management/oversight roles, 23–24
  support for CEOs by, 24
  time commitment of, 30–31
  See also motivation for joining a board

Board position, first 90 days, 169–176
  doing research for, 169–170
  management to oversight mental shift, 170
  observation of boardroom dynamics, 170–171
  onboarding, 172–174
  one-on-one meetings, 175
  preparation for all interactions, 172
  relationship building, 171
  use of strategic input, 171
  work collaboratively, 171–172
Board position, job offer, 157–168
  board contract evaluation, 164–166
  conflicts check, 157–164
  questions to ask, 166–168
  See also board contracts, key areas; conflicts check
Board recruiters. *See* search consultants
Board refreshment, 71
Board-specific skills goal, 152
Boards That Lead (Charan), 157
Body language, 118, 136, 170
Brand roadmap, 53–79
  articulation of unique value proposition, 56–57
  core accomplishments identification, 53–56
  enhancement of online presence, 75–78
  mastery of board-level language, 57–75
  self-owning of brand, 78–79
  setting personal brand goal, 152–153
  See also board-level language
Brown, Wendy O., 81

Business meal interview, 138
Business values, 40–41

Career myths, 2–4
    attending networking events, 4
    board bio creation, 3
    meeting lots of members, 3–4
    need for certification, 3
    previous board tenure requirement, 2
Career "titles"/"types of people," 4
Certifications
    avoidance of mentioning, 87, 92
    myths about needing, 3
    relevance of, 94, 152
Change management, 59
Charan, Ram, 157
Charities, 36, 44
ChatGPT, 15, 77
Chief executive officers (CEOs)
    board member support for, 24
    candidate interviews with, 133–135
    compensation committee and, 71
    initial contacts with new prospect, 3–4
    nomination process, 74
    recruitment of, 22, 34
    relationship-building with, 28, 111, 171
    roundtable groups, 78
    succession planning for, 73, 102
    transition to board membership, 1
Chookazsian, Dennis, 29
CNA Financial, 29
Collaboration, 1, 11, 17–18, 27–28, 55, 61, 64, 102, 113, 144
Committees. *See* board committees
Community values, 40
Compensation committee, 22, 71
Conflict of interest, 59, 70, 161–162

Conflicts check, 157–163
    analysis of financial relationships, 160–161
    conflict of interest policy, 161–162
    document/disclosure of conflicts, 163–164
    existing commitments, 159–160
    key stakeholders, 158–159
    legal/ethical standards compliance, 162–163
Consensus building, 60
Core accomplishments identification
    key role in transformations, 54–55
    risk management, 55–56
    role in business growth, 54
Corporate boards, 34–35
    description, 34
    private company, 35, 129, 173
    public company, 34–35, 40–41, 173
    start-up, 38
Corporate social responsibility (CSR), 58, 60
Credit fund board, 39–40
Crisis management, 10, 23, 60
    board oversight of, 23
    definition, 61
    inclusion on resume (example), 85
    skills development, 10
Cross-functional collaboration, 61
C-suite executives
    reasons for joining a board, 9
    relationship-building with, 111
Curiosity, 29, 176
Cybersecurity, 3, 23–25, 55–56, 61, 145

Decision-making
    active listening/questions and, 30
    board evaluation/interlock and, 70
    data-driven, 141

Index

governance and, 166
high-stakes decisions, 60
influential factors on, 28, 163, 171
risk intelligence and, 89
role of cultural insights, 64
role of effective communication, 28–29
stakeholder considerations, 68
by start-up boards, 38
Diplomacy, 27, 172
Director liability, 72
Directors
    independence of, 34, 39, 72, 74, 175
    liability of, 72
    responsibilities of, 22
Directors and officers (D&O) insurance, 72
Due diligence tips
    capital-raising expectations, 48
    confirming values alignment, 46
    deeper research, 46
    financial/legal responsibilities, 47
    organizational health, 48
    skills fit and contribution, 46–47
    time commitment, 47
Duty of Care standard, 22, 75, 103, 139, 165, 172

Economic Club of Chicago, 73
Education section (LinkedIn profile), 93–94
Egon Zehnder and Korn/Ferry, executive search firm, 130
Email, 1, 84–85, 88, 120, 133, 150, 171
Employees
    comparison to board members, 21, 28
    human resource role, 33
    impact of Enron's downfall on, 26
    as stakeholders, 24
    start-up corporate boards and, 38
Employee stock ownership plans (ESOPs), 42, 85, 128–129
Engagement, 9, 12, 17, 28–29, 40, 54, 68, 76–77, 147
Enterprise risk management (ERM), 62, 88–89
Environmental, social, and governance (ESG), 3, 58, 62, 128
Equity compensation, 13, 73
ESG (Environmental, Social, and Governance) certification, 3
Ethical leadership, 27–28, 162, 163
Ethical oversight, 62
Executive leadership team (ELT), 9, 14, 56, 63
Executive search firms. *See* search consultants

Facebook, 75
Fiduciary duty/responsibilities, 22, 27, 35, 57, 63, 72, 77, 99, 101, 138, 157, 159–160, 164–165
Financial acumen, 40, 63
Financial growth values, 40–41
Financial oversight, 10, 64, 94, 142, 152, 162
Fishbowl, 48
Foundations, 37, 44, 129
Fund boards, 39–41

Gemini, 15
Glassdoor, 48
Global perspective, 64
Goals/goal setting, 151–155
    benefits of defining, 9, 26, 29
    of board relationship building, 86, 113
    board-specific skills, 152

Goals/goal setting (*continued*)
   building rapport with interviewers, 130, 137, 139, 144
   in creating LinkedIn profile, 90
   in developing resume, 84–85
   government credibility goal, 153
   motivation for reaching, 153–154
   networking goals, 152
   personal brand, 152–153
   research opportunities, 153
   role of masterminds in achieving, 78
   seeking a board position (example), 114, 116–117
   short-term *vs.* long-term, 26–27
   SMART goals, 151–153, 155
Governance/governance knowledge, 27, 64–65
Government credibility goal, 153
Growth (value string), 17, 18

Harvard Business Review, 25
Heidrick & Struggles, executive search firm, 130
Helton, Sandra, 21
Hobson, Mellody, 73
Human capital, 27, 65, 94
Hybrid values, 41

Impact (value string), 16, 18
Imposter syndrome, 1
Innovation (value string), 16, 18
Innovative leadership, 66
In-person interviews, 136
Instagram, 75
Integrity, 15, 18, 27, 159, 161, 163, 172
Intellectual challenge (value string), 17, 18
Interviews
   answering open-ended questions, 101
   with board search consultants, 131–135
   body language and, 136
   business meal, 138
   with chief executive officers, 133–135
   in-person, 136
   language substitutions, 99
   leading with who you are, 100
   1-2-1 (one-to-one), 137
   panel, 136–137
   STAR(T) framework and, 139, 150
   types of, 135–138
   virtual, 136
   See also pitch prep strategy
Interviews, preparatory research, 125, 138–145
   employee stock ownership plans, 128–129
   nonprofit boards, 129–130
   online searches, 127
   private companies, 127
   public companies, 126–127
Interviews, questions to ask the board, 145–148
   board alignment, 147–148
   board dynamics, 146–147
   board member expectations, 147
   company growth strategy, 146
   company risk, 146
   nonprofit boards, 148
Interviews, questions to prepare answers for, 138–145
   board dynamics/stakeholder management, 142–145
   financial and risk oversight, 142–143
   governance/leadership experience, 139–142
   industry and strategic insight, 143–144
Intimidation, feelings of, 4, 137

Index

Job offer. *See* board position, job offer
Jones, William "Bill," 110

Kensington International, executive search firm, 131

Legacy building, 9–10
License/certifications (LinkedIn profile), 94
LinkedIn
  creating a newsletter for, 78
  education/license and certifications, 93–94
  exploration of, 48
  headshot/photo recommendations, 87, 90–92
  name/headline/about section, 92–93
  profile, 53, 81, 84–85, 87, 92–93, 114, 130, 153
  skills/recommendations, 94–95
  specialties section, 93
  URL inclusion on board bio, 84
  usefulness in networking, 112

Materiality, 66
McKinsey reports, 25
Mergers and acquisitions (M&A), 34, 54, 66, 152
Motivation for joining a board, 8–14
  compensation, 13–14
  giving back, 9
  influence and power, 11–12
  learning and personal growth, 10
  legacy building, 9–10
  making an impact, 8–9
  making connections, 11
  proprietary survey findings, 8
  relevance and purpose, 10–11
  status, prestige, credibility, 12

tax advantages, 13
travel, 12–13
Moynihan, Kerry, 7, 131
Mutual fund boards, 39–40

Name/headline section (LinkedIn profile), 92
Networking/networking events, 4, 109–122
  advice on seeking advice, 79
  benefit of content posting, 75–77
  board membership and, 11, 29, 47, 98
  case studies: description/findings, 114–121
  description of, by senior executives, 109
  LinkedIn and, 112
  myth related to, 4
  nonprofit board membership and, 103
  professional network description, 37
  relationship building role, 110–113
  role in candidate recruitment, 134–135
  setting networking goal, 152
  when to approach others, 121
Nominations
  board committees, 11, 14, 71, 74, 93, 111
  nomination chairs, 111
  process, description, 74
Nonprofit boards, 13, 35–37
  charities, 36, 44
  foundations, 37, 44, 129
  industry association, 36–37, 145
  interview prep research on, 129–130
  professional association, 36–37, 44

Nonprofit boards (*continued*)
   professional network/clubs, 37, 44, 124, 150
   questions before choosing, 35–36

O'Malley, Jim, 131
Onboarding, 74, 133, 135, 144
   board information, 174–175
   company information, 173–174
   first 90 days, 172–175
One-on-one meetings, 112, 135, 175
One-to-one (1-2-1) interview, 137

Panel interviews, 136–137
Photo recommendations (LinkedIn profile), 87, 90–92
Pitch prep strategy, 97–105
   description of board experience, 102–103
   do's, 103–104
   finding areas you would impact, 101–102
   language substitutions, 99
   leading with who you are, 100–101, 103
   research of your audience, 100
   showing confidence, 98
   things to do, 103–104
   things to not do, 99, 104
   translating expertise into relevant value, 99–100
   See also interviews
Preparation
   for board interview, 125–130, 138–145
   for board meetings, 30, 47
   for executive search consultant interviews, 130–135
   as key to success, 2
   of personal brand, 53–78
   of pitch to board, 101, 104, 116–117
   See also brand roadmap
Private company, corporate boards, 35, 129, 173
Private equity (PE) operating partners, 112
Problem-solving, 10, 17, 175
Professional network/clubs, 37, 44, 124, 150
Profit and loss (P&L) responsibility, 67
Proxy statement, 67
Public company, corporate boards, 34–35, 40–41, 173

Questions
   to ask about nonprofit boards, 129–130, 148
   to ask about private companies, 127–128
   to ask at interviews, 145–148, 150
   to ask when getting an offer, 166–168
   to clarify one's own values, 14–15, 35–36
   open-ended questions, 101
   at panel interviews, 137
   to prepare answers for, at interviews, 125–126, 138–145

Recommendations section (LinkedIn profile), 94–95
Recruiters. *See* search consultants
Reddit, 48
Regulatory knowledge, 67
Relationship-building
   with board members, 111
   with chief executive officers, 28, 111, 171
   with C-suite executives, 111

Index

in the first 90 days, 171
in networks, 110–113
with search consultants, 111, 125
Respect (value string), 17, 18
Responsibilities of board members
  director, 22
  fiduciary, 22, 27, 35, 57, 77, 99, 101, 157, 164–165
Resume, 53, 57, 83–87, 109, 130, 132
Retirees, on boards, 7, 10–11
Risk appetite, 23, 68
Risk management, 23–24, 68
Robert's Rules of Order, 23
Russell Reynolds Associates, executive search firm, 130

Scientific advisory boards, 38
Search consultants
  building relationships with, 125
  description, 111, 130–131
  information/documents required by, 82–87, 102
  interview process, 131–135, 150
  LinkedIn profile and, 87, 92–94
  preparation for interviews, 138–145
  questions to ask, 145–148
  relationship-building with, 111, 125
  steps in the process, 125–133
  types of interviews, 135–138
  use of networks for, 134–135
Securities and Exchange Commission (SEC), 39, 162
Service-oriented values, 40
Shareholder activism, 68
Skala, Cathy, 97
Skill set, for being on a board, 1
Skills section (LinkedIn profile), 94
SMART goals (Specific, Measurable, Achievable, Relevant, Time-bound), 151–153, 155

Social media
  cleansing of online presence, 75
  exploratory research on, 48, 127
  online searches, 127
  personal brand goals and, 152–153
  See also Facebook; Instagram; LinkedIn; Threads; TikTok; X; specific sites
Specialties section (LinkedIn profile), 93
Spencer Stuart, executive search firm, 130
Stakeholder engagement/alignment, 68
Stakeholder resolutions, 69
STAR(T) framework (Situation, Task, Action, Result, Takeaway), 139, 150
Start-up corporate boards, 38
Strategic advisory boards, 103
Strategic oversight, 41, 55, 69, 86, 95
Strategic thinking, 21, 26–28, 41, 137, 143, 175
Stream of consciousness approach (unedited brainstorming), 16, 18
Subject matter expertise, 27, 84, 86, 93, 100, 134
Succession planning, 35, 69, 125

Threads, 75
TikTok, 75
Time commitment, 30–31
Transparency (value string), 17–18

Values, identifying/defining, 14–19
  business/financial growth, 40–41
  chart, example, 15
  community/service-oriented, 40
  four questions, 14–15

Values, identifying/defining (*continued*)
   hybrid, 41
   role in due diligence, 46
   value strings, examples, 16–18
Value strings, 16–18
   authenticity, 16
   growth, 17
   impact, 16
   innovation, 16
   intellectual challenge, 17
   respect, 17
   transparency, 17–18
Venture capital (VC) firms, 112
Virtual interviews, 135, 136
Virtual meetings
   don'ts, 149–150
   do's, 149

X, 75

www.ingramcontent.com/pod-product-compliance
Lightning Source LLC
Chambersburg PA
CBHW072005070526
44583CB00015B/1348